How to Be
Your Own Contractor

New Edition

Remodeling
Additions
Alterations
Building a New Home

Paul H. Rauch

Brick House Publishing Company
Andover, Massachusetts

Copyright © 1988, 1984 by Paul H. Rauch
All Rights Reserved
No part of this book may be reproduced in any form without written permission of the publisher, excepting brief quotations if credit is given to author and publisher.

No patent liability is assumed with respect to the use of the information contained herein. While every precaution has been taken in the preparation of this book, the author and the publisher asssume no reponsibility for errors or omissions. Neither is any liability assumed for damages resulting from the use of the information contained herein.

Library of Congress Cataloging-in-Publication Data

Rauch, Paul H.
   How to be your own contractor: remodeling, additions, alterations, and building a new home/Paul H. Rauch—New ed.
      p.   cm.
   Includes index.
   ISBN 0-931790-74-3 (pbk.)
   1. House construction—Contracts and specifications.
   2. Building—Contracts and specifications.   I. Title.
TH4815.5.R38 1988   88-6986
690'.837—dc19   CIP

CONTENTS

    Introduction   vi

    Remodeling   1
        Inspect Existing Building
        Determine Demolition Costs
        Determine New Construction Costs
        Total Cost Estimate for Remodeling
        Cost-Plus Agreements
        Financing
        Remodeling Activities and Concerns

    Additions   7

    Alterations   8

STEP 1 **Preparing for the Project   9**

STEP 2 **Selecting Your Lot   11**
        General Location—like where you look   11
        Avoid unexpected expenses   11

STEP 3 **Obtaining Financing   17**
        Getting acquainted   17
        How to get the best loan   17
        Presenting the project   19
        Construction progress draws   19

STEP 4 **Preparing House Plans   21**
        Sources of house plans   21
        Working with your architect   22
        What plans and specifications shoud include   23
        Checking plans—what to look for   27

STEP 5 **Developing a Construction Cost Estimate   29**
        Accurate estimate is essential   29
        How to develop a construction cost estimate   30
        Contingency percentage   30
        How to determine the total cost of the project   30

STEP 6 Subcontractors 33

    Definition of a subcontractor 33

    Scope of responsibilities and activities 33

        Excavating and grading contractor 34

        Concrete contractor 35

        Plumbing contractor 35

          Water well drillers

          Septic tank systems

          Automatic lawn sprinkling systems contractors

        Framing contractor (rough carpentry) 39

        Finish carpentry 40

        Roofing contractor 40

        Airconditioning and heating contractor 41

        Electrical contractor 41

        Masonry contractor 42

        Sheet metal contractor 42

        Glass and glazing contractor 43

        Insulation contractor 43

        Stucco and plaster contractor 43

        Drywall contractor 44

        Cabinetmaker contractor 44

        Painting contractor 44

        Miscellaneous contractors 45

STEP 7 Selecting Subcontractors 47

    Search for subcontractors 47

        Long-time resident of the area 47

        Medium-size communities 48

        Large cities—no knowledge of contractors 48

    Desirable subcontractor qualities 49

    Accumulating reference information 49

    Obtaining bids 50

    Evaluating bids and selecting subcontractors 52

STEP 8 Construction Schedule 55

    Chronological construction outline 56

STEP 9	**Construction** 59	
	Prearrangements 59	
	Daily activities 60	
	Conclusion 69	
Appendix A	**Insurance** 71	
	What and why 71	
	Title insurance 71	
	Liability insurance 71	
	Builder's risk policy 71	
	Workman's compensation insurance 72	
	Owner-builder as employer 73	
Appendix B	**Building Permits** 75	
	Working with inspectors 75	
	How to apply for building permits 75	
Appendix C	**Subcontractor's File Cards** 83	
Appendix D	**Common Construction Terms** 85	
Appendix E	**Cost Control Accounting 89**	
	Simplified accounting system 89	
	Construction progress draws 89	
	Waiver of lien 90	
Appendix F	**Samples of Bid and Contract Forms (Proposals)** 93	
Appendix G	**Builder's Request for Construction Advance** 95	
Appendix H	**Construction Cost Estimate** 97	

INTRODUCTION

Owner-builder contracting gives you the opportunity to step into the shoes of a general building contractor and build your own house. There are advantages to be gained if you are willing to accept the responsibilities. Perhaps the most important is the opportunity to save money.

A general building contractor must charge at least 10 percent above actual building costs to stay in business. He has to pay for his office, equipment, employees, insurance, taxes, license, advertising and all the other expenses of running a business. Expenses you will not have as a one-time, owner-builder contractor.

In addition, most general contractors make a profit. To do that they tack on 20 percent or more to their estimated building costs. Is it unreasonable for the owner-builder to expect to save 20 percent? Worth thinking about, isn't it?

A licensed general building contractor knows how to put it all together and get the work done by subcontractors. That is important. The fact that you are reading this book shows that you know how really important it is. Who is going to tell you how to do it? Do you have enough confidence in yourself to believe that with the proper guidance you can do what others are doing?

The emphasis here must be on *with the proper guidance*. Undoubtedly you are aware that the do-it-yourself approach to owner-builder contracting by an inexperienced person can be a devastatingly rough road—unless that person has proper guidance. This book was written to provide the information and guidance that makes it possible for you to undertake and successfully complete the construction of a new home for yourself. It starts with the first things you need to know and carries you through the entire building process. With this information and the step-by-step instructions at hand, you will be able to handle with confidence all the details and decisions that are required.

This book will show you how to get work done by others through subcontracting. (It will not teach you how to do the work yourself.) It is written with the expectation that you will put yourself in the position of a general building contractor and assume his duties and responsibilities, although your legal title will be owner-builder contractor. You will benefit from the author's 32 years of contracting experience as a licensed general building contractor. This information will not harm well qualified general building contractors, but it will certainly help those who want to build their own homes. It will save heartaches, frustrations, and financial loss for many who want to do their own contracting but who could easily get hurt by not knowing the important details.

Acting in your capacity as owner-builder contractor you have several options open to you. One is to have all the physical tasks done by various subcontractors, involving yourself only in the planning, managing, coordinating and communicating necessary to get all the work done through other people. Or you may be handy with tools and already know one or more of the trades involved in building a house. In this case you may decide to subcontract only those jobs you cannot do yourself.

Again, you may choose to subcontract most of the work but fill in the odd jobs yourself or with help from your family and friends. Being your own building contractor gives you flexibility to make whatever arrangements best fit your situation.

Usually the general building contractor first comes into the picture after the owner has obtained house plans and made arrangements for financing. However, since this book is written as a guide to owner-builders, it includes the total package: the acquisition of the lot, obtaining building plans, arranging financing, the complete step-by-step performance of a general building contractor from the moment he is handed the house plans until he provides the owner with a notice of completion.

No license is required for you to be an owner-builder contractor, but one word of caution. The law permits you as owner to build your own house by entering into contracts with all the subcontractors you need and to perform all the other functions of a licensed general building contractor. However, *the law does not permit you to act in this same capacity to build for anyone else.* Only a licensed general building contractor can do that. Even though this book will be of great value to you in the construction of your own house, the possession of it in no way implies or suggests that you may, or should, become involved as a contractor for others.

You may find, though, that you have discovered a whole new and exciting future for yourself. After building a home you may want to continue to enjoy the excitement of the construction business and to become a licensed general building contractor. The knowledge you obtain from this book and the experience you gain by building your own house may be one great step toward a future profession.

Remodeling, Additions, Alterations

Although the prime concern of this book is the building of a new house, the information and guidance given can be adapted to remodeling, addition and alteration projects. However, there are additional problems that may be encountered by the person undertaking changes to an existing structure. The three major classifications of such changes are defined in order to clarify the differences. How best to handle the various problems is dicusssed for each classification.

Remodeling may be defined as extensive rework of an existing building in order to improve its appearance and usefulness. The remodeling may require rearranging the interior: removing walls, adding walls, installing new fixtures, reworking the exterior, restructuring or building a new roof, and possibly reworking the foundation. Remodeling usually requires extensive demolition of the existing building.

Additions require very little rework of existing buildings and may be almost entirely new construction. They are undertaken to provide additional rooms or to increase room sizes and make other improvements.

Alterations are usually defined as rework of existing walls, windows, roof, exteriors, etc. The work involved is usually much less than that in either of the other two classifications.

Many areas throughout the country require that you obtain a building permit if the changes you propose to make will alter the structure or appearance of the building, or if the cost exceeds a specified amount. Also, if the building is located in a community where an architectural control committee (or similar organzation) exists, you will be expected to submit your plans for remodeling or additions to that committee for approval before work begins.

Insofar as practical, the subjects in this handbook are presented in the same sequence as the events occur. The primary subjects covered are listed in the table of contents.

Remodeling

Remodeling frequently requires the dismantling and removal of a considerable portion of an existing building in order that many changes may be made. The new structure that will replace the old may be built by the conventional methods used for any new building. However, there are problems that differ from ordinary new con-struction that need to be recognized by the owner-builder.

Perhaps the first difficult problem will be to determine the estimated cost of the project. Getting a reasonable estimate of the total cost before beginning construction is essential in any building project.

In remodeling there are many unknowns that will be encoun-tered in the partial destruction of an existing building and in rebuilding it. Estimating the cost of removing unwanted sections, without damaging the structure that is to be reused, is not an exact science.

Also, questions arise that may not be fully answered until walls are opened up and conditions revealed, such as:

Were those areas of the building that are to be reused built to code, or will they have to be brought up to existing code?

Will examination of the plumbing, wiring, etc., reveal that much of it will have to be replaced?

Will it be possible to find subcontractors who will give a fixed-price bid on the job or, considering all the unknowns, will they take it only on a cost-plus basis?

Is cost-plus a reasonable arrangement?

The following suggestions will aid you in obtaining a cost estimate that should provide assurance that the job can be done for a predetermined price.

To obtain the information you will need, it will be necessary to open inspection holes in various areas in order to see the actual conditions.

1. Inspect the Existing Building

Most cities and counties require that any portion of the old building that is to be part of the new structure must be brought up to code. It will be necessary to inspect the construction of the existing building in order to determine the costs of bringing it up to code. You will need to determine the answers to such questions as:

Are foundation footings and stem walls sound and of adequate dimensions to accommodate the remodeled building?

Are there indications of termite infestations? All infested lumber must be removed and replaced for the new structure.

Are sewer lines and water lines in good condition and plumbed according to the latest code? Will they need repair or replacement?

Is the electrical wiring up to code at the service entrance, circuit-breaker panel, and throughout that portion of the house that will remain a part of the remodeled building?

Is the construction of the floors, walls, ceilings and roof as required by the latest codes? Walls with 2x4 studs on 24-in. centers may not be acceptable. Most areas now require 2x4 studs to be on 16-in. centers.

Do the span and spacing of floor joists, ceiling joists and roof rafters meet code specifications? The roof structure must be adequate for the type of roof you will be installing. It may not be the same type as the existing roof.

After determining the extent of the repairs and replacements that will be necessary, you will need to estimate, as closely as possible, the costs involved. This may not be easy, as even experienced craftsmen cannot always predict what they will find when they open up old walls. The more experience a craftsman has had with remodeling, the more capable he will be of determining accurately the costs that will be incurred.

With that in mind, try to find electricians, plumbers, etc., who have had remodeling experience. They may not be willing to give you a firm bid, but they should be able to give you a reasonably close estimate for the work you will need done in order to comply with current building codes.

2. Determine Demolition Costs

These costs may be separated into three activities to insure more accurate cost estimates:

a. Labor and equipment rental costs to tear down portions of the existing building.
b. Labor costs to store and protect reusable items and materials.
c. Labor and equipment costs to clean up and dispose of rubbish.

Do not "ballpark" these cost figures, as these expenses usually exceed expectations significantly. Estimate each category. Then total your estimated costs for these three items to obtain your demolition cost.

Tear down

Determine as precisely as possible the areas of the building to be demolished or removed. Select items to be carefully removed for reuse. Discuss with contractors the various methods to be used. Obtain bids from insured licensed subcontractors to do the tear-down and demolition work. Detail in the contract the extent of the work.

Store and protect

Make a list of the items to be removed, stored, and protected for future use. Determine where and how they will be stored. Include an adequate allowance for the costs involved in handling, transporting, storing, and restoring to usable condition.

Clean up and dispose

The quantity of rubbish generated will most probably surprise you. Attempt to determine the volume of rubbish by sizing up the areas of the building that will be torn down. Contact a rubbish disposal company to obtain their price per cubic yard for pickup and disposal. Do not forget to add in your costs for on-site labor to collect the rubbish into a pile for pickup. On a sizable demolition job expect the cleanup to be an everyday job for several days.

3. Determine New Construction Costs

For the new construction on your remodeling project, you may obtain valid cost estimates in the same manner as described for new construction in other chapters of this book. Obtain bids from the various subcontractors you will need.

Total Cost Estimate for Remodeling

Develop a total cost estimate for your remodeling project by adding the totals from items 1, 2, and 3 above. To that total add a contin-gency allowance of 10% to cover the unexpected and overlooked costs that may occur.

The complete cost estimate will also provide you with reference information when you are arranging with the various subcon-tractors for their services. By having prepared your estimate meth-odically and realistically, you will have usable guidelines for discussing reasonable dollar amounts with subcontractors. Some tasks may be well defined and suitable for fixed-price contracts. Others, for which the extent of the work to be performed is difficult to determine, may require cost-plus agreements.

Cost-Plus Agreements

If you enter into cost-plus agreements (sometimes called time and material agreements) you may find the following suggestions helpful.

Avoid arrangements that require you to pay the subcontractor, or any of his employees, a weekly or monthly fixed fee for "supervision." These are sometimes called "retainer fees."

Supervisory costs are normally incorporated into the hourly rate you will be paying. You should pay for job performance and not for passing time. If you agree to a retainer fee, you will be providing a strong temptation to slow down your job. For the subcontractor, it becomes "more months, more money." Retainer fees are common in cost-plus contracts. Look out for them. Don't be taken in.

Require that hourly pay rates for each craft and machine be stated in the agreement. Require careful daily time-keeping on all employees and equipment.

State in the agreement the percent of markup permitted above the subcontractor's costs for materials, supplies and fixtures.

Require copies for your review of all billings before writing checks for these items. Keep copies for your files.

State in the agreement that the contractor is required to discuss all major purchases with you *before* he orders the items. Check for yourself the going prices on the items and require that they be purchased from sources that will provide them at lowest cost. Remember that a subcontractor working on a cost-plus basis is not motivated to keep costs low. In fact, he is constantly tempted to buy the higher priced items. The higher the price, the more his profit percentage will be.

Be sure that all materials ordered and billed to your project are delivered to and used on your job. This includes ready-mixed concrete, lumber, roofing, bricks, plumbing, nails and many other generally used items that are easily misappropriated. Also, observe the usage of materials and watch for waste. However, do not be so concerned about saving materials that your crafts people lose time, which could cost you more than the wasted materials.

Cost-plus agreements must be properly prepared and reasonably controlled if they are to be a fair and satisfactory arrangement for all parties concerned.

Financing

Financing a remodeling project is not very different from financing a new house. Use the procedures for financing new house construct-ion beginning on page 17 of this book.

Remodeling Activities and Concerns

In many areas weather is an important factor to be considered when scheduling your project. Avoid the rainy season or cold weather, if possible. Either one will greatly increase the time and expense to protect the house adequately after you have opened it up during demolition and rework.

It is particularly important to protect those areas and items that are to be reused in the remodeled house. As the owner-contractor you will have to assume the responsibility for seeing that temporary protective coverings are installed. Also, let the subcontractors know that you expect them to do all they can to reduce the exposure time and to help provide the necessary protection.

When selecting your subcontractors choose those who have a reputation for getting their jobs done quickly. That attribute is particularly valuable when remodeling.

The removal of items to be reused in the remodeled house should be done carefully and with the realization that things can be damaged if not stored properly. Wood and metal products should be stored in a cool and dry area where there is sufficient room for the items to be stored neatly and safely.

Wood pieces should not be laid flat directly on concrete floors. Place 1x2s or 2x4s approximately three feet apart on the concrete floor to support flat wooden pieces, doors and windows. These items may also be stored standing upright if they are well supported.

Doors or windows may warp unless stored with the top edge flat against a wall or other support. Be careful that door knobs, hinges and other protrusions do not place the items in a position to warp while in storage. Store cabinents and other built-up items with the base flat on the floor and with no twist or warp in the face frame or top. Use plywood to protect windows from accidental breakage.

Tearing down existing structures generates safety hazards. Perhaps the most dangerous, and easily overlooked, are rusty nails that protrude from lumber recently pulled apart. If boards with nails in them are lying around they seem inevitably to be turned so that the nails stick up. Also, tossing sticks with protruding nails into a junk pile can rip fingers. A rusty nail puncture is a prime tentanus hazard.

Before cutting into or breaking down walls, ceilings or floors be sure the electrical power to the area is shut off at the fuse box or circuit breaker panel. Also, turn off gas and water lines at their main shutoff valves. Take the time to make the work activities and areas as safe as possible.

Reconstruction

When your remodeling project gets to the reconstruction stage, your task of directing, coordinating and communicating with subcontractors will not be too different from any new construction work. Refer to the directions given for new construction in this book to guide you through your remodeling construction period.

Additions

The building of an addition to a house is almost entirely a matter of new construction. The areas of connection to the existing structure will generally require some removal of exterior wall and roof coverings to expose the structure of the building in order to make the tie-ins. The demolition work should done carefully in order to avoid unnecessary expense.

It is important to the future value of the house that the new addition not be easily identified as an addition. The new portion should be designed and detailed to be similar to the existing house. Use roofing and exterior materials that are identical to, or compatible with, those that exist.

The removal of any part of the existing roof and the opening of walls should be carefully planned in order to keep the exposure to weather as short as possible. Frequently the new structure can be well along before it is necessary to open the existing building to make the tie-ins.

Unlike the problems involved in remodeling, developing a cost estimate for an addition is a relatively routine process. The guidelines given for new construction in this book will serve you well for an addition project. Review the information in the book on subcontractors (Steps 6 and 7) and determine which crafts you will need for your addition. The activities and extent of work required from each of the subcontractors should be defined. Firm bids and reasonable contracts should not be difficult to obtain. It should not be necessary to go cost-plus on a new addition.

Develop your own construction schedule to accomodate the extent and specifics of your addition. The time factors will most probably be much shorter than for a complete new house for each stage of construction, but the sequence of events should be similar to those given in Step 8 in the book.

Financing

Perhaps the easiest financing for additions are the home equity loans now available from many banks and savings and loan companies. Most banks using this method of financing have quite open requirements regarding the accounting methods you use for keeping track of expenditures on the project. You should, however, monitor those expenditures carefully to make sure that the project will be completed within your projected cost guidelines.

Alterations

The term "alterations" generally applies to relatively minor changes to a building. These changes may include anything from changing the size of a window to converting an attached garage to a family room. There will be no major demolition as in remodeling, nor will there be new construction as in making additions to a house.

Alterations may require three or four different crafts, such as carpentry, painting, plumbing and electrical work, but it may be difficult to find subcontractors who are willing to take small alteration jobs.

One alternative is to engage individual craftsmen for each job. Such people frequently work a regular daytime job and do small jobs during off hours and weekends. However, unless they are licensed to be subcontractors, they cannot enter into a valid contract with you; in the eyes of the law they will be your temporary employees. Check your insurance policy to see that you are properly covered for this contingency.

You may get lucky and find a "jack of all trades" who is skilled in all the various crafts you need. Sometimes these handymen also have subcontracting licenses, allowing you to sign a contract with them for the job.

Preparing a cost estimate for alterations may not be easy, as you probably cannot expect to get bids for such small jobs. Perhaps the best approach is to list the materials you will need and get prices. Add to the materials cost a reasonable labor cost at the wages pre-vailing in your area. This should give you a rough idea of what your project will cost.

Suggested financing for an alteration project is the same as for an addition: a home equity loan, which is relatively easy to get and does not usually have stringent project accounting requirements on the part of the lender.

STEP 1

Preparing for the Project

Building a new home is an exciting experience. However, it is easy to understand why a person would give long and careful consideration to such a project before taking on, for the first time, the responsibilities for the actual construction of a house. If you have not built before, it is only natural to be concerned about those responsibilities and activities that you know little about. But they do exist and you will need to cope with them.

This book describes the details of everyday activities so that even if you have very little knowledge of how to build a house, you can nevertheless successfully organize and supervise others who are the construction specialists.

It will not be necessary for you to be able to do any of the many specialized construction jobs. You need only know how to get others who have the expertise, knowledge and experience to do those jobs. These experts, or subcontractors, are available. You will learn from these pages how to obtain their services. Also you will be shown how to plan, organize, communicate and direct the activities of the subcontractors so that you may successfully construct your own home.

Even though there will be many decisions to make and actions to take, each within itself, taken at the right time and with the information you will have at hand, will be an easy step. That time-honored cliche "Inch by inch, anything is a cinch" is still true. You need only follow the instructions and take the actions as clearly described in the following chapters. (For additional reading, *Before You Build: A Preconstruction Guide,* Ten Speed Press, 1981, by Robert Roskind is suggested.)

Take the time as you go along to attend to the details as set forth even though they may seem insignificant to you. Later you will discover their importance. In order to keep instructions clear and to the point, insignificant details have been omitted and nonrelevant comments avoided.

Take your first steps

1. Turn to the table of contents and follow the subjects through the entire

sequence of events as suggested by the chapter titles. This quick look will give you some feeling for the scope of the project and the help you can expect from this book.

2. Read the book through lightly. Do not try to understand in depth each and every paragraph. Do not try to anticipate all the actions and decisions that you think might be required at any one time. This first look is an overview to set into your subconscious mind the overall project. You can work out the details later when you take each step in its time and order.

3. Proceed with the project by carefully studying each step in turn. Take actions as instructed. Refer to the text as frequently as necessary to ensure that your activities are correct and complete.

STEP 2

Selecting Your Lot

The task of selecting and purchasing a lot should be approached with a good foreknowledge of what is really essential. You will need to look at more than the beauty of the lot to ensure that you are buying a good building site that is well suited to your needs.

General location—like where you look

Observe the life style of the people and the general quality of the homes in any location you are considering. Would you enjoy or be at ease with the community?

Picture the house you want to build. Does it fit well into the neighborhood? You will want to avoid building a large and expensive home in any neighborhood where most of the existing houses are much smaller and of much cheaper construction. The reason is that such a neighborhood will depress the value of your house in the event you decide to sell in the future. On the other hand, do not build a cheap, small house in an expensive area. You will not only be very unpopular in your new neighborhood, but you may also find, in the event you decide to sell, that the sale will be hurt by the comparison of your house to the quality of the others in the community.

A flat, level lot in good soil and above the street is desirable. It will: be easy and less expensive to build on; place the house in the best relationship to the street; provide good soil for landscaping. A steep lot or one that requires grading, excavating, or fill will cost more to prepare for the construction. Generally speaking, such lots are less expensive to buy, which helps pay for the extra bulldozer work. House plans for such lots may cost more as the architect may find it necessary to spend more time *fitting* the house to the terrain. However, unusual lots frequently present more opportunities for the design and construction of novel and interesting houses.

Avoid unexpected expenses

Having found a lot that you like and that appears to fit your needs, you should carefully check and be assured that all of the following practical conditions are right. Do not enter into a purchase agreement without either positive proof that these conditions are right or specify in your purchase agreement that the purchase is contingent upon these conditions being suitable for the construction of your home.

1. Electrical power, domestic water, telephones and an acceptable sewage disposal system must be either on the lot or available close by. If any of the lines for these utilities have to be run any distance to service your lot, you should determine what this will cost you. These costs should be considered as part of the price you are paying for the lot.

2. If sewers are not available, you will need to find out what type of sewage system is approved for the area and if your lot will accommodate it. If you will be using either a septic tank system or cesspool, you will need to know that the soil conditions are suitable for such systems and that the building department will permit their use. A soil percolation test may be required to make this determination.

3. Even if sewers are available, find out how far below the street they are. If they are several feet down and the soil conditions are sandy or excessively wet, special equipment and shoring may be required to make the sewer connection. The cost of the connection may run two to four times normal. A normal connection may cost about $500 but your connection may cost $2,000. Add this difference to the price of the lot you are considering.

4. In some outlying areas you may find that domestic water is not available from a central system. If individual wells are providing the water in that area, be sure that the lot you are considering is large enough to permit proper location of the well and septic tank and that permits for both can be obtained. Also, inquire from knowledgeable people in the area as to the depth required for a good well. Depth determines the cost to a large extent.

5. Storm drains, natural water courses and level of underground water tables should be considered. Study the terrain around the lot you are considering, particularly if it is hilly or near a stream bed that is usually dry. Try to determine the effects of a prolonged and heavy rain or rainy season. Also, and particularly if you are planning a basement in your house, determine if there is ground water at a level that could cause you problems in the basement during the rainy season. If the ground water level rises to 4 or 5 feet below the surface, you are going to have problems with the basement that goes down 8 feet!

6. Deed restrictions, right-of-ways, and easements are common on many lots. Most of these you can live with, but it is important that you read and

understand all of such that pertain to the lot you have under consideration. Do not assume that just because the lot is for sale that it is a buildable lot that will meet all of your conditions and requirements.

If you find a lot that you particularly like and it appears to meet all of the above considerations, you may want to go ahead with the deal rather than take the chance of losing it to another buyer while you are verifying all the important details. The way to handle this problem is to enter into the deal and make a deposit to bind it. Specify in the agreement that the purchase is contingent upon conditions being satisfactory for the construction of the proposed home. The agreement should state that the deposit will be returned in full if the conditions cannot be met within a specified time limit.

Do not permit any work to be done on the lot before you complete arrangements with the loan company. Costly delays in obtaining financing for the construction have occurred simply because someone did not know the complications they were creating by starting work a few days too soon. Many loan companies will not complete arrangements for your loan until they can be assured that the title is clear of any possible mechanics' liens against the lot.

WASHINGTON COUNTY BOARD OF REALTORS
LOTS & ACREAGES CONTRACT FORM

☐ LOTS (Up to 1 acre)
☐ ACREAGES (Over 1 acre)

MLS No. _____
Listing Date _____ Expired Date _____ Geographic Area # _____

OWNERSHIP
Owner: _____
Phone: _____
Address: _____
_____ Zone _____

FINANCIAL
Price $_____ Price per acre $_____
Taxes $_____
Loan Bal $_____
Payment $_____ @ Int ____%
Tax ID No. _____
Lender _____
Additional Encumbrances $_____ @ Int ____%
Payment $_____ Lender _____

ASSESSMENTS (Asses)
1 ☐ Paid (AsPd)
2 ☐ Not Paid (AsNtPd)

PAYMENT INCLUDES (Incl)
1 ☐ Tax (T)
2 ☐ Insurance (I)

EXISTING LOANS (ExLn)
1 ☐ Fm Home (FmHm)
2 ☐ Fed Land Bank (FLB)
3 ☐ Contract (Ctr)
4 ☐ Conventional (Conv)
5 ☐ Second Trust Deed (STD)
6 ☐ All Inclusive Trust Deed (AITD)

TERMS OF SALE (Terms)
1 ☐ Equity (Eqty)
2 ☐ Refinance (Ref)
3 ☐ Contract (Ctr)
4 ☐ Assume (Asm)
5 ☐ Exchange (Ex)
6 ☐ Owner Subordination (OwSub)
7 ☐ Second Trust Deed (STD)
8 ☐ All Inclusive Trust Deed (AITD)
9 ☐ Cash (Csh)

DESCRIPTION
Lot Size _____ Total Acres _____
Cultivated Acres ____ Irrigated Acres ____ Pasture Acres ____
Subdivision _____ Lot No. _____
Water Shares _____ Source _____ $_____

UTILITIES (Utl)
1 ☐ Electricity (Elec)
2 ☐ Propane (Prop)
3 ☐ Water (Wtr)
4 ☐ Sewer (Swr)
5 ☐ Septic Tank (Sptc)
6 ☐ Well (Well)

IMPROVEMENTS (Improv)
1 ☐ Paved Road (PvdRd)
2 ☐ Unpaved (Unpvd)
3 ☐ Curb & Gutter (C-G)
4 ☐ Roll Curb (R-C)
5 ☐ Sidewalk (Sdwk)
6 ☐ Fenced (Fnc)

WATER SHARES (WtrSh)
1 ☐ Owned (OwWtr)
2 ☐ Rented (RnWtr)

VEGETATION (Vegt)
1 ☐ Alfalfa (Alfa)
2 ☐ Oak Brush (OakBr)
3 ☐ Fruit Trees (FrtTr)
4 ☐ Trees (Tree)
5 ☐ Woods (Wood)
6 ☐ Natural Grass (NtGrs)
7 ☐ Pines (Pine)
8 ☐ Aspen (Asp)
9 ☐ Sage Brush (Sage)
10 ☐ Crops (Crop)

TERRAIN (Terr)
1 ☐ Flat (Flat)
2 ☐ Gradual Slope (GrSlp)
3 ☐ Steep Slope (StSlp)
4 ☐ Hilly (Hill)
5 ☐ Mountain (Mnt)

SOIL TYPE (Soil)
1 ☐ Loam (Loam)
2 ☐ Sandy (Sndy)
3 ☐ Rocky (Rcky)
4 ☐ Clay (Clay)
5 ☐ Gravel (Grvl)
6 ☐ Marsh (Mrsh)

AGENT
Firm _____
LO _____ Phone _____
Salesman _____
LS _____ Phone _____
Fee Paid to Selling Office $_____ ____%
(% of gross sales price or flat fee)

REMARKS
(off# ____) This offer is contingent upon the following items: Percolation tests must prove the soil conditions will permit use of septic tank and leach lines for sewage disposal. Written verification must be obtained that all governmental requirements regarding sewage can be met and that permits can be obtained to construct a one-family dwelling. Proof must be provided that electrical power and potable water are available to the lot without additional cost to the buyer for line extensions. The deposit made herewith toward the purchase of this lot shall be refunded in full and this offer cancelled if the above conditions cannot be met within 60 days.

SALES AGENCY CONTRACT
Member of Multiple Listing Service of Washington County Board of Realtors

In consideration of your agreement to list the property described herein and to use reasonable efforts to find a purchaser or tenant therefor, I hereby grant you for the period of _____ months from date hereof, the exclusive right to sell, lease or exchange said property or any part thereof, at the price and terms stated hereon, or at such other price or terms to which I may agree in writing.

During the life of this contract, if you find a party who is ready, able and willing to buy, lease or exchange said property or any part thereof, at said price and terms, or any other price or terms, to which I may agree in writing, or if said property or any part thereof is sold, leased or exchanged during said term by myself or any other party, I agree to pay you a commission of _____% for such sale, lease or exchange. Should said property be sold, leased or exchanged within _____ months after such expiration to any party to whom the property was offered or shown by me, or you, or any other party during the terms of this listing, I agree to pay you the commission above stated.

You are hereby authorized to accept a deposit as earnest money from any potential buyer on the above described property. Said deposit to be held in a trust account.

I hereby warrant the information herein to be correct and that I have marketable title or an otherwise established right to sell, lease or exchange said property, except as stated. I agree to execute the necessary documents of conveyance or lease and to prorate general taxes, insurance, rents, interest and other expenses affecting said property to agreed date of possession and to furnish a good and marketable title with abstract to date or at my option a policy of title insurance in the amount of the purchase price and in the name of the purchaser; in the event of sale or lease of other than real property, I agree to provide proper conveyance and acceptable evidence of title or right to sell, lease or exchange.

In case of the employment of an attorney to enforce any of the terms of this agreement, I agree to pay a reasonable attorney's fee and all costs of collection.

You are hereby authorized to obtain financial or contract information from any mortgagee holding a loan on this property.

You are hereby authorized and instructed to offer this property thru the Multiple Listing Service of the Washington County Board of Realtors.

You are hereby authorized to place an appropriate sign on said property.

City of _____, State of _____, this ____ day of _____ 19 ____

_____ Company _____
                                                                Owner
by _____   _____
        Salesman   Owner

I hereby acknowledge receipt of a copy of this agreement _____
                                                                                    Owner-Acknowledgement

"This is a legally binding form. If not understood, seek competent advice."
Approved Form Washington County Board of REALTORS ®

Illustrated on page 16 is one type of agreement form to be used when making an offer to purchase a lot. The offer becomes a purchase agreement to buy the lot, on the terms stipulated, when accepted by the seller. The purpose of this illustration is to indicate when and how you specify the conditions that must be met to satisfy you that the lot is acceptable to you. Note the typed-in conditions under "Remarks" on the form.

STEP 3

Obtaining Financing

Getting acquainted

Obtaining financing is an important step for you as the owner-builder. As it probably will not be easy, carefully follow the suggested course of action.

Preliminary discussions on financing should be one of the first steps taken after you have decided you want to build your own house. In these first inquiries you should not get into specifics of the project but rather gather information about the various lending institutions in your locality. You will need to know: what are the current interest rates; what *points* the banks and savings and loan companies are charging; what terms apply under various conditions; how much time is allowed for construction under the construction loan agreement (usually six months); amount of the monthly payments and the number of years for the repayment of the long-term mortgage loan; what information the lender will need from you.

During these first discussions you will want to be prepared to discuss in general terms: the approximate size of the house you expect to build; the location; approximately what you expect it to cost. From this general information the loan officers should be able to give you a fair idea of the percentage of the cost of the construction that they will be able to finance under various circumstances.

During these preliminary discussions, *do not* state that you are intending to act as your own contractor. Also, do not attempt to tie down any firm commitments. *You are not prepared at this time* to provide the information that the loan officer will need *to properly evaluate you or the project* that you propose to undertake.

How to get the best loan

It is advisable to shop around at several banks and savings and loan companies in your area. You will probably find a wide variation in what the different institutions will do. The amount of money available to loan varies considerably almost daily. This constantly changing condition makes for wide differences in responses and terms. Be sure to make sufficient contacts to know where you can get the best deal.

After you have assembled all your facts and figures (more about that later), you will be better able to present your proposition. In effect, you must be prepared to *sell* the loan officer on your project: your financial ability to meet your part of the cash requirements of the project; your future ability to meet the monthly mortgage payments; the value of the completed house; and most of all, your ability to act as your own contractor. The better the whole package looks to him, the better the arrangements he will make.

Lending institutions are reluctant to make construction loans to owner-builders. Perhaps the most important reason for this is their concern regarding the completion of the house in good order and with no clouds on the title. A house that gets into financial difficulties after it is well along but cannot be completed by the owner-builder becomes a disaster to the lending institution. They suddenly find themselves with a monster on their hands that cannot be sold or occupied and which does not produce monthly payments toward the mortgage they hold.

Too frequently owner-builders tend to underestimate the cost of the building. First, because they are inexperienced, they will plunge into the project *without preparing a comprehensive cost estimate based upon valid first-hand information.* Secondly, they overestimate the savings that their own labor will provide. They reason that they can do some of the work themselves and thereby save cash outlays. This is true to some extent, however, these savings are frequently overestimated. Unless a valid cost estimate is prepared an owner-builder may overextend himself. Before he has completed the job, he may find that he is in serious financial difficulties and has an unfinished house on his hands.

On the other hand, the bank does not take these risks when the building is being constructed by a licensed general building contractor. In most states the contractor is required to be bonded to amounts sufficient to assure the completion of the building. In addition, a licensed general building contractor has an established reputation that can be checked by the bank.

Confidence in the general building contractor is an important factor influencing loan officers to give preferential treatment to him. They have confidence in his ability to manage the project well, complete the construction in good order and in a reasonable time, and to avoid any financial complications. With this understanding of the bank's position, you, as the owner-builder contractor, can be prepared to cope with this problem. They will want assurance that you know what the costs will be and that you are fully qualified to manage the financial details as well as the actual construction.

Presenting the project

Make the following preparations so that what you do and say will illustrate your capabilities when you go to make the financial arrangements for the construction of your house.

- Talk at length with many subcontractors as discussed later so that you will become better acquainted with the construction business. Learn to talk the construction language.

- Develop a reasonably accurate construction cost estimate of the project as detailed in Step 5.

- Put together a work schedule (using the information in Step 8) to guide you.

- Know what your own cashable resources are and determine how much you want from the lending institution.

- Prepare a financial statement on the forms provided by the bank or savings and loan company.

- Take a complete set of professional quality house plans with you when you go to make arrangements for your loan.

Construction progress draws

In your discussions with the loan officer you will have the opportunity to learn how his company prefers to handle its payouts for the construction expenses. Two arrangements are most commonly used, with variations. The following brief descriptions will acquaint you with the basics of each.

Under one arrangement the construction funds remain in the custody of the bank and they make the payments for expenses incurred for the construction of the house. As the owner-contractor you will receive the bills from your various suppliers and subcontractors. You will submit these bills to the bank and they will issue the checks to each supplier or subcontractor. (See Appendix G.)

The other arrangement, which for many years was the more common, is for the bank to issue *construction progress payments* to the contractor (or owner-builder contractor). These payments are for a percentage of the total loan and are made upon verification that a specified construction stage has been completed. It is the responsibility of the contractor to pay the construction bills as they come due. It is not unusual for the bank to require verification that the bills are being paid.

It is very important to you, as well as to the bank, that no mechanics liens are filed against the property. The title must be clear at the end of the construction in order for a smooth transition to your long-term mortgage loan.

The above construction stages are usually as follows:

- Foundation completed   25% draw
- Framing completed   25%
- Finish carpentry completed   25%
- Occupancy permit issued   25%

Sometimes the final payment is not released until thirty days after the notice of completion has been filed. This provides additional time to assure that no mechanics liens are outstanding.

The lending institution may require that you deposit with them the difference between the amount they will loan and the estimated cost of construction. This is to assure them that finances will be available to complete the project.

The bank will require fire insurance on the house during construction as well as for the house when completed. This, of course, is something you would want anyway.

STEP 4

Preparing House Plans

Complete, professional-quality house plans and specifications are essential. The value to you of well designed and detailed plans cannot be overstated. The process of preparing house plans develops the character, size, type and other essential details of the house you will eventually live in. Many people, from cost estimators to construction workmen, will study and work with the plans. Each will use them to determine all the details and dimensions of the house in order to build it as it is shown on the plans. If the house is to be built right, the plans must be right.

Sources of house plans

There are several ways to obtain plans for your house. Many people prefer to arrange with an architectural designer who specializes in homes to prepare house plans for them. There are several advantages to a custom designed house. Perhaps the most important is that your own particular preferences can be realized. In the following pages are specific suggestions how to work with a designer in order to obtain plans that are designed to suit your particular needs and preferences.

But first you may want to consider some of the alternatives. There are hundreds of ready-made plans available at very reasonable prices. As a source of ideas the ready-made plans are fantastic. As for practical application, the use of such plans presents some problems. It is difficult to find a plan from the catalogs that meets all of your own personal preferences. Also, there is the problem of fitting a design to the lot you have chosen in order to make the best use of its natural advantages.

If you find a ready-made plan that you like and that can be built on your lot with only minor changes, you can make those changes in red pencil. Be sure that any change made on one sheet is also made on all other views or floor plans that may be affected. If the changes you want in the ready-made plans affect the structure to any great extent, then probably most of the sheets will have to be changed. This should be done by an architect to avoid errors that could be costly if not found until construction is well under way.

You may be qualified to draw your own plans. If you have experience in building houses and working from architectural plans you would already have a working knowledge of what is required on a good set of plans. You would also need some drafting experience to know how to make good drawings on vellum that will produce readable prints. Also, you will need some knowledge of building codes and structural requirements.

If you are capable of preparing drawings that are comparable to the average plans available, certainly you may wish to do your own house plans. But you should avoid the fallacy of thinking that you do not need good, complete, well drawn plans just because you are expecting to act as your own contractor.

Working with your architect

If your lot is a conventional city lot without any unusual features, it may not be necessary for the architect to see it. However, if the lot is a view lot or on a hillside, if it is unusual in shape or otherwise presents special problems and considerations, it would be advisable to encourage the architect to visit the lot with you. He needs to see your lot and its surroundings in order to design the best possible house for the location.

Try to visualize with the architect the most appropriate style, size and shape of a house for your lot. If you have a view lot be sure to discuss window sizes and locations. Discuss single floor, split-level, and two-story houses. Let him know your likes and dislikes about various styles of houses. You may have pictures or plans of houses you like. These visual aids will help communicate your preferences to the architect.

Architects have pictures, plans and brochures showing construction details, cabinets, turnings and other special treatment ideas. They also have illustrated brochures showing plumbing and light fixtures, appliances, floor and wall coverings, exterior sidings and veneers and other features that may be incorporated into the design of your home. Ask to see these when discussing specific details. Use the illustrations, photos and drawings as a means to communicate your preferences.

Give your architect leeway to come up with original ideas. Consider carefully his suggestions. Generally he will have good reasons for his arrangement of the details. Reserve the final decisions for yourself after carefully considering the various options.

The size of the house will be determined to a large extent by: Location, as discussed in Step 2; Lot size, shape and character; Cost, how much you want to spend or how much is available.

Of course you will discuss room sizes with your architect. You will have to decide which are going to be larger and which smaller. Their combined floor space has to fit into the size of the house as determined by considerations outlined above.

As the designer works with the floor plans he will use your suggestions and his best judgment to work out arrangements and room sizes. Let him know your preferences but also let his experience guide you. In his profession he is constantly in touch with current trends and knows what appeals to many people. A home is a more valuable asset if it can readily be sold when necessary.

Give considerable thought to the exterior appearance of your house. Let the architect know that you want a beautiful home, not just any house. The basic cost of a house will be much the same whether it is a simple unattractive group of rooms under one roof or whether thought was given to make it attractive by careful attention to proportion, details and the right combination of exterior materials. A beautiful house is a better investment.

Your architect should provide you with a complete set of plans and specifications. These become a vital part of your contracts with the subcontractors. The plans and specifications will provide the specific information that the subcontractors will work to in their construction of the house. What they see on the plans and in the specifications is what you will get. Take the time to thoroughly study and understand the house plans yourself. Question the architect on anything you do not understand or approve.

What plans and specifications should include

A complete set of house plans should include detailed drawings, to accurate scale, showing the following:

- Plot plan
- Floor plan
- Basement and foundation plans
- Front, side, and rear elevations
- Detail sheet showing:
    - Wall-section detail
    - Kitchen and bathroom cabinets—front and side elevations
    - Linen closets, bookcases, paneled partitions, fireplaces
    - Window and door schedules

Plot plan

The plot plan is usually drawn to 1/10" or 1/16" scale and should show:

- Property lines of the lot accurately and fully dimensioned
- The name of the fronting street
- Street width and dimension to the center of the street
- Street address of the lot
- Legal description (lot number and subdivision number, or name)
- Location of any easements
- Arrow indicating north
- Scale of drawing
- Location of any existing buildings, structures and driveways
- Proposed buildings, structures, retaining walls and driveways
- Septic tanks and leach lines (if any)
- Existing and proposed site drainage

Hillside plot plans may also require:

- Topographical map of the lot
- Location of retaining walls (if any)
- Typical retaining wall section cut showing construction details
- Vehicular access to public road, plan and profile views

Floor plans

Floor plans are usually drawn to 1/4" scale (1/4" = 1 ft.). They should clearly show the size, shape, and location of all rooms, halls, closets, cabinets, entries, patios, porches, garages, doors, windows, fireplaces, etc. The drawings should be fully dimensioned to provide detailed and definite information for the construction of the building.

Floor plans should also show:

- Location of electrical lights and outlets
- TV and phone outlets
- Power vents

- Plumbing fixtures (tubs, showers, sinks, toilets, water heaters)
- Kitchen and laundry room appliances
- Heating and airconditioning equipment locations
- Wall, ceiling, and floor types, textures, and finish materials
- Skylight locations

Basement and foundation plans

Unless the foundation is unusually complicated, the basement and foundation plans can be combined as one drawing. The general requirements are the same as for the floor plans. In addition the foundation plans should indicate the footings and stem walls, their dimensions and other structural requirements.

Front, side, and rear elevations

These elevations should be drawn well and complete enough to convey a good picture of how the constructed house will look. There is seldom any need for extensive dimensioning of the elevation views. However, the grade, floor and ceiling heights should be shown, as should the roof pitch and chimney height. Roofing and exterior materials should be shown and described.

Detail sheets

Kitchen and bathroom cabinets should be detailed with front and side elevations shown. All critical dimensions should be given. Special items such as bookcases, linen closets, fireplaces and paneled partitions should be detailed and dimensioned with front and side elevations shown. A wall section should be shown giving wall construction details and dimensions. Frequently insulation information is referenced here.

Window and door schedules

Schedules for each of these items should be shown. The windows and doors should be described in detail and identified by letters (for windows) and numbers (for doors) showing their locations on the floor plans.

General specifications

Either the plans or specifications should call out specifically the following items in order that your subcontractors know exactly what they are agreeing to provide and can bid accordingly.

1. The specific quality and capacity of the heating and airconditioning equipment. As the owner-builder it would be advisable for you to learn as

much as you can about the various makes and models of heating and airconditioning equipment. Visit the dealers that sell these products and accumulate brochures that will give you specific details that you can use to identify exactly what you want. Include this descriptive information in the specifications.

2. The specific size and type of water heaters. Also, indicate the size and kind of water pipes to be used throughout the house.

3. The make and model of the water softener (if water is hard).

4. The R factor of the insulation in the walls, floors and ceilings should be specified. To conserve energy, the following are recommended as minimum R factors: walls R-19; floors R-22; ceilings R-38. In many localities the building codes have not been updated. The minimum R factors required by the code in your area may be considerably less than those shown above. You are only required to meet the minimum specified in the code, but the additional insulation is a good investment.

5. The kind and quality of roofing materials should be called out either on the plans or in the specifications.

6. Specific information should be provided on bathroom fixtures giving color, type, size and quality. Also specify the manufacturer as quality and colors (with the same name) may vary.

7. Built-in kitchen appliances should be specified by make, model and color. Visit appliance stores and determine what best suits your needs. Pick up the literature that gives the specifics you will need to properly identify the items on your specifications sheet.

Subcontractors frequently have connections where they can buy appliances at a discount. They seldom pass this discount along to the owner-builder. Of course they will prefer to install these appliances in your house. They may try to sell you on these substitutions. Be sure that they meet your requirements and qualifications. Otherwise insist that the subcontractor supply the items as specified.

Or you may wish to have your subcontractors submit two bids—one including the appliances and the other without. In this way you can determine what prices you are really paying for the appliances through your subcontractors. Watch the ads of big volume appliance dealers and know what you can buy the items for yourself. You may find that you can buy on sale for less than the subcontractor's prices even though they give you their discounted price.

Checking plans—what to look for

After the architect has completed the original vellums, you will want to carefully study them before he runs the blueprints.

Following is a list of items to check on the plans before you accept them. Changes can readily be made by the architect at this time. The same changes, if not made until construction is under way, could be expensive. Study each room separately on the floor plan and visualize how you will arrange the furniture in the room. Next determine if the following items are located in the room so that they are most convenient and to the best advantage.

1. Window locations and sizes. Consider sunlight, ventilation and drafts. Most people like airy rooms, but some do not like to have a draft across their beds. Also consider the view from the window. Is it a picture window? Or is the view to be shut out?

2. Light switches and wall outlets. Are any switches behind doors when they are open? Use three-way switches generously for convenience. Are light switches located where you want them?

3. Check door locations and direction of swing. Also, check for your preferences of sizes and types of doors.

4. Check the number and locations of phone and TV outlets. Be sure that there are enough of them. A phone outlet by the toilet may be a great convenience.

5. Study the stairways. Seven-inch risers and 11-inch treads are standard. Six-inch risers and 12-inch treads are frequently used for the more graceful and formal stairways. Avoid steep stairs even for the back stairways to basements as they are dangerous. Any stairway for a residence that is steeper than one with 8-inch risers and 10-inch treads is not recommended. Head clearance above the stairs is important. Six feet eight inches above the outer edge of the tread is recommended as a minimum distance.

6. Is the type of floor or floor covering indicated? Particularly check such areas as the front entry, foyer and bathrooms where the type of finish floor may make a difference in the subfloor construction.

7. Are the wall coverings, textures or panelings indicated? Are they what you want? The drywall contractors or plastering contractors will need to know which walls to texture and also where to apply a smooth finish.

8. Check out the type ceilings shown for special rooms such as the living room, dining room, family room and master bedroom. Cathedral ceilings, open beam, sloped or other special ceilings should be noted on the plans.

9. Carefully study the floor plans of the kitchen and the detailed elevation views of the kitchen cabinets. A good architect will probably have your kitchen arrangements well thought out. Be sure they serve your personal preference.

10. Study the room sizes and compare them to rooms you know. (Take measurements in existing rooms, if actual dimensions are not known.) Particularly study the small rooms such as bathrooms, walk-in closets and hallways. A bathroom, or hall that is six inches too narrow can feel very cramped and less than satisfactory. The same six inches taken from the adjoining room may never be noticed.

The architect will make the changes you request and complete the plans and specifications. After you have given your final approval, he will have blueprints made from the vellums. Usually the architect keeps the original vellums. You should request a minimum of eight sets of prints.

Expect the architect to charge a fee that may be approximately 1 to 2 percent of the estimated cost of construction of the house. This is not a hard and fast rule. Prices vary greatly in the various regions of the country. Inquire around in your area and get some idea of what the established architects are charging. Be careful of those who offer to do the plans at bargain prices. What you get may be so incomplete as to cost you much more in construction costs and rework.

STEP 5

Developing a Construction Cost Estimate

Accurate estimate is essential

To ensure that you will have adequate finances to complete this project successfully it will be necessary for you to develop a cost estimate that is as accurate as possible. How to do this will be described in detail here and in Steps 6 and 7.

You will need this information when applying for the construction loan and in determining the feasibility of the project. The amount you can borrow plus the cash you can make available must equal, or exceed, the estimated total cost. Later you will use your Cost Estimate when reviewing bids from subcontractors, letting contracts, making trade-off adjustments and in the overall monitoring of the financial aspects of the project.

The very nature of contracting provides a certain degree of flexibility in allocating funds. Overruns must be balanced by reduced costs in other areas. You will find it necessary to make decisions regarding trade-offs in order to make available funds cover all cost commitments. Keeping the expenditures within funding capabilities is very important. The monitoring of costs must be a top priority right from the beginning. If early costs are permitted to run over budget when money seems plentiful, meeting the final bills can become a nightmare.

The flexibility in expenditures is limited to what can be accomplished by trade-offs. Following is an example of a trade-off:

> After the rough framing is nearly completed, you decide that one room needs another window. The framing subcontractor makes the change and bills you for the additional cost. To offset this expenditure, which was not in your cost estimate, you will need to downgrade or eliminate some other item. To do this, you may choose to use cedar shingles for the roofing instead of the more expensive thick-butt shakes you had originally expected to use.

How to develop a construction cost estimate

As you study the construction cost estimate work sheets (Appendix H), you will quickly realize that the development of a realistic cost estimate is an important and time consuming step in your construction project. Be prepared to take all the time and patience necessary to do the job right.

You will need firsthand information from many sources in order to correctly fill in the necessary data on the work sheets. Every item must be considered and accounted for with an accurate amount written in under the Bid or Cost column (column 1).

In order to obtain this information you will need to contact banks, utility companies, the Department of Building and Safety, contractors, material suppliers, appliance stores, suppliers of plumbing fixtures, electrical fixture stores, and other sources of materials, supplies and services. From these contacts and activities you will be able to obtain the facts and figures necessary to accurately complete the cost estimate sheets.

Of course it will be necessary to have complete house plans and specifications to submit to the subcontractors in order to get their bid prices to include in this estimate. More about how to obtain bid prices is described in the following chapters.

Contingency percentage

General building contractors have found that, regardless of their extensive experience and careful attention to detail, it is necessary to include in their estimates a *contingency* item to cover unexpected expenses or an accumulation of small overlooked expenses. If you believe that your estimated cost figures are quite accurate you should include a contingency figure of not less than 5 percent of the total costs. If it has been difficult to obtain relatively firm prices on several of your costs, you should use 10 percent as your contingency figure and add that to your total.

How to determine the total cost of the project

The first use of the construction cost estimate is to determine the total cost of the project. To do this you will:

1. Make the contacts and obtain the information for column 1 (Bid or Cost).

2. You will total all cost figures in column 1 for all pages of the cost estimate and enter that total in the space provided on Work Sheet No. 3 under column 1.

3. Determine your contingency percentage by following the suggestions made in the previous paragraph, Contingency Percentage, and enter that figure after Contingency on Work Sheet No. 3.

4. Multiply the total cost figure by the contingency percentage and enter the result in column 1.

5. Add total cost and contingency cost together and you will get the total estimated cost of project.

The second use for the construction cost estimate work sheets is to record the names of the contractors who are awarded the contracts. Later you may complete your records by entering the check number and the date when the contract is complete and the contractor paid. Also you will want to enter the actual amounts paid and the dates when items are purchased or services paid for.

You will find that your construction cost estimate is a good reference when you are making arrangements that commit you to a cash outlay. By referring to the original estimate for that item or service shown in column 1, you will know if you are staying within your budgeted allowance.

Monitor all expenditures by comparing them to the original amount you entered in column 1 and, if any overruns occur, decide what other expense you are going to eliminate or reduce to pay off the overrun amount.

Do not permit yourself to ignore overruns or pass them off as being covered by the contingency allowance. The contingency should be considered as a last ditch reserve that will only be used when all other means of covering overruns, or unexpected expenses have been exhausted.

STEP 6
Subcontractors

Definition of a subcontractor

Although subcontractors are actually contractors, the term is used in the construction business to identify and separate out from general contractors all the *specialized* crafts and trades that are involved in the construction of a building. Under the owner-builder contractor arrangement, no general (overall) contract exists. Therefore the term "subcontractor" might be considered inappropriate. Nevertheless, it seems advisable to stay with the common usage of the term and refer to the specialized contractors as subcontractors.

Perhaps the most meaningful contribution you will make toward the successful construction and completion of a home for yourself is the selection of the subcontractors and your relationship with them. These are the prime responsibilities you are accepting that are normally borne by the general contractor. How you succeed in the important activities of planning, scheduling, coordinating and communicating with the subcontractors will be the measure of your overall success. Your personal initiative, ability and good judgment in selecting and managing your subcontractors will be a big factor in how well the operation progresses. Securing good, reliable subcontractors is a task that is time consuming. But its importance to the overall success of the project makes it well worth expending much time and effort.

Scope of responsibilities and activities

Most people who have not been involved in building construction do not know what areas of work performance should be expected from each subcontractor and what responsibilities each should assume. A brief description of each of the subcontractor classifications will aid you in your search for good subcontractors. Later you will find this information useful when you are working out the contracts with your subcontractors. Also it will help you supervise the activities of the subcontractors as they perform their work on your project.

The information below describes: what is normally expected of each craft or service; how one craft interfaces with another; how to avoid having two subcontractors include the same work in their bids; how to avoid having some task or materials missed with no one providing them. The following contractor classifications are presented in the same order as the normal sequence of construction events.

Excavating and grading contractor

Contractor shall provide supervision, equipment and operators to perform normal building site excavating, grading, backfilling, dirt hauling, stump and rock removal, etc. to accomplish the following:

- Level the building site
- Excavate for the basement, footings and foundation
- Excavate for septic tanks and sewer connections*
- Dig trenches for water, sewer and leach lines*
- Dig storm drains

The excavating and grading contractor shall backfill excavated areas after the sewer, water lines and septic tanks have been installed and areas around the basement after it has been constructed and sealed. He may also include the finish grading in his contract, however, this will require his crew to return with the equipment several weeks later when the building is nearing completion. You may save money by having the landscape contractor do the finish grading. Your contracts with the contractors should specify your intentions.

If your house has no basement and the lot is level, your excavating and grading will be minimal. A separate excavating contract will not be necessary. Your concrete contractor can dig his own footings and the plumbing contractor can arrange his own excavating. It is not too unusual to find that the concrete contractors are equipped to do their own excavating and grading and prefer to bid accordingly. This has the advantage of having only one contractor responsible and sometimes the operations are coordinated better.

In all cases the excavating contractor and the concrete contractor should work very closely and cooperate well to assure the construction gets off to a good start.

*This work may also be done by other contractors such as a sewer and septic tank contractor or plumbing contractor. Determine which works best in your situation and define the extent of work to be accomplished on each contract.

Concrete contractor

- Contractor shall supply all materials, equipment, forms, concrete, labor and supervision necessary to provide the concrete work as required by the house plans and specifications.

- He shall lay out, form, reinforce and pour house and garage footings, stem walls, foundations, floors, driveways, sidewalks, steps, planters and retaining walls.

- He shall provide all the reinforcing rod, anchor bolts, post bases, reinforcing wire mesh, etc. necessary to complete the concrete work as specified.

- He shall ensure that: all footings are in native soil or soil compacted to meet code requirements; concrete mixes and reinforcing meets specifications; all slab floors are well finished, smooth, flat and level (or to the grade specified).

- He shall bear the burden and expense of assuring that the concrete is properly cured and protected from freezing.

- He shall provide concrete pumping and water pumping as necessary for the completion of his work in a reasonable time.

- He shall backfill around basements, foundations, etc. as necessary to provide suitable work areas for the other crafts. (Or this work may be done by the excavating contractor. Determine which contractor will do this and indicate it on the contracts.)

Plumbing contractor

The scope of the plumbing contractor's activities and responsibilities vary greatly depending upon whether he lives in a small community or a large city. A small town residential plumbing contractor probably includes the widest variety of work in his normal activities. He may consider, as his normal scope of work, all of the following activities:

- Sewer connections to city sewer lines
- Septic tank installations and leach field construction
- Cesspool digging and construction
- Rough and finish plumbing in new residences including:
  - Sewer lines in the house
  - House to street, or to septic tank, sewer lines
  - Domestic water lines and gas lines

- Installation of water heaters, softeners and filters
- Supplying and installing tubs, showers, toilets and sinks
- Heating and airconditioning including:
  - Fabrication and installation of air ducts systems
  - Air handling units, freon condensers, heat pumps
  - Gas, oil and coal furnaces
  - Evaporative coolers
- Digging wells, supplying and installing water pumps
- Installing automatic lawn sprinkling systems
- Plumbing repairs and sewer system cleanout

On the other hand, the larger the city (usually), the greater the specialization. You will find the broad spectrum of plumbing activities are subdivided into several independent specialized contractors such as:

1. Sewer contractor
   - Confines his work to making sewer connections to city sewers.
   - Provides his own backhoe for excavating.
   - Cuts the city street blacktop and excavates down to the sewer.
   - Taps the city line and installs a short sewer line which extends on to the owners private property.
   - Backfills over the connection leaving the capped end of the sewer line exposed.
   - Patches the paving in the street.
   - Makes all arrangements with the city for permits and inspections.

2. Sewer tank and cesspool contractor
   - Limits his activities to the following:
   - Excavates for cesspools, septic tanks and leach lines.
   - Supplies and installs septic tanks, leach lines and cesspools.
   - Backfills over the septic tank, leach lines and cesspools.

3. Plumbing contractor (rough and finish)

    - Supplies material, labor and supervision to install sewer and water lines in the house. Runs main line from water meter to house. Installs water regulator.

    - Runs the exterior sewer lines and makes the connection to the stub-outs which were installed by others.

    - Supplies and installs water heaters, tubs, showers, toilets and sinks (or he will install these items if supplied by the owner).

    - Arranges with a water softener company to install a softener (or the owner can make his own arrangements).

4. Heating and airconditioning contractor

    - Specializes in heating and airconditioning.

    - Fabricates and installs air ducts and air handling units.

    - Supplies and installs airconditioning condensers or heat-pumps.

    - Supplies and installs furnaces.

    (More on this subject under heating and airconditioning contractor.)

5. Water well drillers—specialized contractor

6. Water pump dealer and installer—specialized contractor

7. Lawn sprinkling systems contractors—specialized contractor

How you handle your plumbing contracts will depend very much upon the availability of specialized contractors in your area. Also, of course, on what public utilities are available to your lot. In most cases it will probably be to your advantage to obtain separate bids as follows:

1. Plumbing contractor (rough and finish)

    In addition to the activities and responsibilities outlined above under Plumbing Contractor you should include the work listed under Sewer Contractor.

    Miscellaneous items the plumbing contractor should supply as part of his contract include the following:

    - Roof jacks for all vents that penetrate the roof.

    - Laundry dryer exterior exhaust vent.

- Washing machine wall panel with faucets and drain.
- Pressure regulator on the water main—installed downstream from the main shutoff valve at the house.
- All flexible tubing, angle valves, etc. needed to connect water heaters, softeners, sinks, lavatories, toilets, etc. to lines.
- Faucets for the kitchen sink, laundry sink, bath lavatories, tubs, showers and hose bibs. These items might not be part of the plumber's contract unless you specifically include each item and give manufacturer and model number. Makes, models, sizes and finishes vary greatly in price and each item should be fully identified if included in the contract. You may wish to buy these items yourself if you have a bargain source.

The plumbing contractor may or may not wish to do his own excavating. Clarify this situation between the contractor that will be doing the excavating and the plumber so that they do not both include that cost in their bids.

2. Heating and airconditioning contractor

Contractors specializing in this field are usually better qualified to properly design and install these specialized systems. (More airconditioning details are given later under the title Airconditioning and Heating Contractor.)

3. Water well drillers

Water wells, when required, and the pumping systems probably should be on a separate contract, not part of the plumbing contract.

4. Septic tank systems

Contractors specializing in septic tank systems usually are more proficient than others to which this function may only be a sideline. If you do let this as part of the plumber's contract you may find that he simply contracts this out to a septic tank contractor and adds his percentage to the price. In either case it may be to your advantage to have a separate contract for the septic system.

5. Automatic lawn sprinkling systems contractors

These contractors usually provide well designed systems for less money.

Much of the work can be done by less skilled (and less expensive) workers than plumbers.

From this review of the many aspects of plumbing (and all the related activities that plumbers generally consider to be part of their business—sewer systems, all water systems, heating and airconditioning) it is obvious that you have a choice of several ways to subcontract for these essential tasks. After getting acquainted with these contractors in your area, you will be able to determine what arrangements will be best for your particular situation.

Framing contractor (rough carpentry)

Contractor shall supply all material, labor and supervision necessary to complete the rough framing of the house as shown on the plans and specifications. He shall supply all the lumber, beams, posts, insulating sheathing, plywood, exterior siding and roof trusses necessary to complete the rough carpentry of the house and garage. Also, he shall supply all hardware needed including joist hangers, flashings, bolts, nails, steel beams, stanchions. His scope of work will begin with the attaching of the mudsills to the foundation and continuing until the following items have been completed as described:

- He shall construct the floors, stud walls, ceiling and roof structure.
- Walls and ceilings shall be ready for interior wall coverings (drywall, plaster or paneling), and exterior walls ready for painting, masonry veneer or stucco.
- Floors shall be ready for carpeting, vinyl, tile or other floor coverings.
- Roof structure shall be sheathed and ready for finish roofing materials.

Roofing is usually let as a separate contract. If not, require the framing contractor to assume all the responsibilities outlined under Roofing Contractor. Soffits and fascia boards shall be installed by the framing contractor unless a separate contract is let for metal soffits, fascia and rain gutters. Metal flashings for the gutters on the roof may be supplied by either the roofing contractor or the framing contractor. Clarify this on your contracts so that both do not include these costs in their bids. Or each may expect the other to provide and install these items and no one does. This kind of minor oversight can cause an expensive delay when the roofing crew comes on the job if they are expecting the flashings to have already been installed. The roofing crew will be delayed until the flashing material can be obtained and installed as the flashing must be in place before the roofing is laid.

Your contract should be specific in stating that the framing contractor shall supply and install the garage doors and the automatic door opener, if any. Doors and openers vary greatly in style and price. Describe each correctly on the contract or in your specifications.

Contractor shall supply and install the front entry door and hardware. Also, the other exterior doors. All doors should be specifically and fully described in the plans and specifications.

He shall install (but not necessarily supply) the prefabricated windows and frames. He shall construct built-in window frames for any field-glazed stationary windows. Usually field-glazed windows are installed by the glass company that supplies them. Clearly state on the contract if the framing contractor is to supply the prefabricated windows.

Finish carpentry

Finish carpentry may be a part of the framing contract or it may be a separate contract. The contractor shall supply supervision, labor and materials to complete such items as the following (not necessarily limited to these items, check your plans):

- Install interior door frames, doors and hardware.

- Install door casings, baseboards, base shoe, picture moldings, chair railings, special paneling, stair treads and risers and railings. (Discuss with the rough and finish carpenters which will be responsible for the stairway structure.)

- Finish carpenter will install: wardrobe doors, shelves and clothes poles; fireplace mantels; soffits; decorative wall paneling. (He may build linen closets, drawers, shelves and doors but be sure to have a clear understanding between the finish carpenter and the cabinetmakers on such items as these. Be specific in identifying who will be responsible for these items.)

After talking with the cabinet makers and finish carpenters you will be able to decide which items you will want the cabinetmakers to build and install. Better cabinet work, drawers, etc. can be made in a cabinet shop than on the job where power tools are limited and working conditions are less than ideal.

Be specific in writing your contracts in order to avoid overlapping or missing any items. Know for sure what you expect from each crew.

Roofing contractor

Contractor shall supply supervision, labor, equipment and materials, including such items as building felt, shakes, shingles, roofing tile, asphalt shingles, or hot-rolled roofing, depending upon the type of roofing specified.

Items that may also be needed include metal flashings for gutters, metal roof saddles, caps, etc. These can be supplied and installed by three different contractors—framing, sheet metal or roofing. Specify in the contracts who will provide and install the sheet metal items. Sewer vent roof jacks usually are supplied by the plumber (see Plumbing contractor) and installed by the roofing crew.

Attic ventilators that are roof mounted and skylights should be installed before roofing begins. These should be obtained well in advance and installed by the framing contractor at the time he lays the roof sheathing.

Airconditioning and heating contractor

Correctly engineered systems with the components properly sized provide quiet airflow evenly distributed throughout the house with relatively stable air temperatures. Oversized condensing units will short-cycle causing increased maintenance costs and higher power consumption. They also create cold drafts when the unit is on due to the oversized unit being able to chill the air too rapidly. Undersized air ducts create high velocity airflow and make it difficult, if not impossible, to correctly balance out the system and obtain an even distribution of air throughout the house.

Contractor shall provide supervision, labor, and material to install the heating and cooling equipment necessary to properly heat and cool the house as specified on the plans and specifications. He shall design, construct, and install air-duct systems as well as supply and install air handling units, condensers, heating units, or heat-pumps, and furnaces as specified. Concrete pads for the condensing unit, or heat-pump, shall be provided by the concrete contractor.

The design may call for subfloor ducts, or they may be considered desirable by the contractor. In this case it will be necessary for this part of the duct system to be ready early in the project and installed before the concrete slab is poured or before sub-floors are installed on the floor joists of raised floors.

Close coordination and cooperation will be necessary between this contractor and the concrete contractor and the framing contractor. Also, be sure the electricians are informed of the size and location of airconditioning and heating units requiring electrical power.

Electrical contractor

Contractor shall provide material, labor and supervision to install all electrical wiring, switches and outlets as shown on the plans. This will include electrical service to airconditioning units, washers, dryers, water heaters, power vents, garage door openers, ranges and ovens. He shall supply and install specified electrical heaters, power vents, smoke detectors, door bells, intercoms and light fixtures. (You will want to select the specified items and describe them in the contract by make, manufacturer's number, size and color.)

Contractor shall supply and install the service head, meter panel and circuit-breaker panel. He shall also supply and install TV cables to locations shown on the plans.

Arrange with the phone company, or include in your electrical contract, for the installation of phone lines. They should be run before the insulation is put in and the drywall installed.

Masonry contractor

Contractor shall provide supervision, labor and materials to construct masonry walls, veneers, fireplaces, stove surrounds and hearths as shown on the plans and per the specifications. You should become familiar with—and select before the materials are ordered—the colors, sizes and textures of bricks, stone, cultured stone, slumpstone, concrete blocks and the mortar needed on your job.

Contractor shall provide any supporting angle iron required, wall ties, metal flashings and re-bar for chimneys, metal fireplace forms, firebrick and flue liners. Some types of mantels (wood, precast stone) and some types of hearths (tile, precast stone) may be supplied and installed by other than the masonry contractor. Be sure you cover the costs someplace and specify which contractor will supply and install.

The concrete contractor is responsible for the footings and foundations for fireplaces and planters. As such, there must be close coordination between the concrete contractor and the masonry contractor.

Sheet metal contractor

The use of sheetmetal for soffits and fascia is becoming increasingly more popular. Precoated metals withstand adverse climatic conditions better and require less frequent repainting. New techniques in forming and installing provide very attractive appearances. Specialized contractors with special installation equipment are the most qualified to do this work. They also install rain gutters to match.

The contractor shall supply supervision, labor, materials and the equipment to install these items. Coordinate this work carefully with the framing crew and the roofing contractor. The framing crew must have the structure completed to the point where the fascia and soffits can be installed. Then the fascia should be installed for the roofing crew to work to.

Sheet metal fabrication jobs such as clothes chutes and special flashings can be made by the airconditioning duct fabricators or any general sheet metal shop, not by the specialized soffit and fascia men.

Glass and glazing contractors

Glass contractors and window supply houses will give you bid proposals for all your window and glass needs. Prefabricated window units (combination windows and frames) vary greatly in quality and price. You will need to compare the quality and prices of various manufacturers and be sure you know what you want. The bidders should be specific in the descriptions of what they will supply at the prices they are quoting. The more elite companies build such expensive windows that they can only be justified for expensive homes. However, there are a number of manufacturers that build good moderately priced units.

The supplying contractor should deliver the windows and glass items but he may or may not install them. Most generally the framing contractor installs the window units. However, field-glazed stationary windows should be installed by the supplying glass company. Glass shower enclosures, glass doors and mirrored wardrobe doors are usually installed by the supplying glass company. Determine whether the framing contractor or the glass contractor is to install the windows and write your contracts accordingly.

Insulation contractor

Contractor shall supply and install insulation in all areas specified in the plans and specifications and to the R values required. Fireproof heat shields or materials shall provide protection around all heat sources that penetrate ceilings (bathroom heaters that are ceiling mounted, recessed spot or flood lights). Window boxes and similar areas are easily overlooked by the insulation crews. Be sure they are included in the job. Insulation (cellulose) in bathroom walls helps deaden bathroom noises.

Stucco and plaster contractor

Contractor shall supply supervision, labor and materials to stucco all exterior areas specified on the plans and to building codes. He will supply and install metal lath, corners and base screed where required. He shall supply and install building felt and wire over the wall sheathing which will have been previously installed by the framing contractor. He shall mix and apply the stucco coats with the finish coat in the color you select.

Interior plastering is seldom done any more, but in some areas interior lath and plaster craftsmen are still available. It makes a better wall—

straighter, more fire resistant, and more sound deadening, but more expensive.

Drywall contractor

Contractor shall provide labor, supervision and materials (sheetrock plaster panels, joint tape, joint compound, fasteners, metal corners and texturing compound) to complete drywall installing, taping and texturing per plans and specifications.

If radiant heating is to be installed in the house the drywall contract shall specify that the laminated electric ceiling shall be included. Also the contract should specify if the garage, basement and stairway are to be drywalled. The drywall contract should also include acoustic ceiling installations where specified on the plans.

Cabinetmaker contractor

Contractor shall supply supervision, labor and materials to construct and install specific cabinets, closets and other items as specified in the contract. The cabinets and other items shall be constructed as detailed in the plans and as agreed upon with the owner-builder after he has seen the various styles and woods that the cabinetmaker can supply. Field dimensions shall be taken by the contractor to ensure that all the items, whether shop built, purchased or built-in, shall fit properly when installed.

You, the owner-builder, shall decide which items the cabinetmakers will be responsible for and which will be built-in by the finish carpenters. Both contracts should itemize the items that each is responsible for. Usually the cabinetmakers build and install all items that can be built better in a cabinet shop.

Many factory-built kitchen cabinets and bathroom lavatory cabinets are good quality. They are factory finished and available in many stains and painted colors. These can be installed by the finish carpenter. They usually cost less for similar quality than custom built cabinets. If you expect to use factory-built cabinets, be sure that the architect designs the kitchen to accommodate the standard sizes of cabinets that are available in your area. Also, the framing contractor must be careful to hold kitchen and bathroom (where applicable) *finished measurements* to the dimensions shown on the plans.

Painting contractor

Contractor shall provide materials, labor, equipment and supervision to paint the interior and exterior of the house per the plans and specifications and to the colors you select.

The finish grading should be completed outside and most of the finish carpentry work inside should be completed before the painter begins. The finish electrical and plumbing work should await the completion of the painting. Wall papering, carpets and drapes follow thereafter.

Miscellaneous contractors

The activities of the remaining contractors listed on the construction cost estimate sheets are quite straightforward and confined to their specialty. After you have dealt with the major contracts and contractors, it is doubtful that you will need a separate description of the activities and responsibilities of these minor contractors. Therefore these classifications have been omitted from these detailed descriptions.

STEP 7

Selecting Subcontractors

Search for subcontractors

Individual circumstances will, to a large extent, dictate the problems involved in obtaining good subcontractors. These circumstances fall into four broad classifications, which may be defined as follows:

1. Those who have lived in one community for several years and are already well acquainted with many of the contractors in the building trades.

2. Those living in a medium-sized community which has only a few contractors in each classification. You may not have a personal knowledge of the contractors you will need.

3. Those living in large cities where many subcontractors are available but your personal knowledge of them is very limited.

4. Those who are new to an area and must start from the beginning and develop the neccessary knowledge of all the subcontractors that will be needed.

Long-time resident of the area

If you have been living in your community for several years, you probably already know many of the building subcontractors. Selecting subcontractors will be relatively easy. You may already know their reputations with customers and suppliers and the quality of their work.

If you know them personally and know that they are honest and reasonable in their prices, you may not need to ask for competitive bids. If you are only acquainted with them and do not know them personally you most probably will want bids from more than one subcontractor. The least a competitive bid can do is help avoid unnecessary expenses due to someone's unintentional error. Also, they are helpful in assuring that you are paying a reasonable price for what you are getting.

In some smaller communities you may not have much choice. There may be only one qualified plumber, electrician or whatever. However, your protection in that case is the very fact that the community is small and the contractor has to live with the people he does work for.

Medium-size communities

There is one aspect of a medium-size community that is difficult to deal with. Sometimes where there are only a few contractors in each classification they protect each other by being very independent about submitting competitive bids. If you let them know that you are asking for other bids on the same work, they may simply refuse to give you a bid. They may even act indignant and accuse you of implying that they are untrustworthy. This attitude is really a coverup, but you have to live with it.

The best approach to this problem is to make enough inquiries regarding the contractors to satisfy yourself that you know which one has the best reputation for quality workmanship and honest dealing. Get that contractor to submit a bid to you.

Large cities—no knowledge of contractors

The search for subcontractors should begin almost as soon as you have decided to build yourself a house. As you have seen in the previous chapter, it requires a surprising number of different trades and services to build a modern house. And since, in many cases, it is advisable to obtain at least three bids for the more expensive jobs, you will be contacting many people. This will take time and effort.

As mentioned before, you are taking on the responsibilities of a general contractor. Certainly one of the prime attributes that a general contractor brings to his job is knowledge of his subcontractors. This knowledge you will need to acquire in a short time.

Your search for subcontractors can begin with the Yellow Pages of your phone directory. Look under the classifications of the various trades and services. Phone and arrange to talk to several subcontractors in person. Watch their crews at work whenever possible. Ask for references and visit the people you have been referred to.

Watch for houses under construction. Visit these job sites and observe the crews at work. Inquire as to who the subcontractors are. Make appointments and visit them. Inquire at lumber yards, building supply houses, paint and glass stores, banks and other businesses that frequently have contact with the subcontractors. Usually they will know their reputations. Most will be cooperative and willing to recommend contractors they believe to be best qualified.

Desirable subcontractor qualities

Of course you want men who turn out good work, but in addition to that, try to determine if the subcontractor is reliable. Will he: keep his commitments? Get his crews on the job on schedule? Push the job along in good time? Be a capable and energetic craftsman? Pay his bills promptly? Frequently a contractor who has a high rating with one company or supplier will also be well recommended by others.

When you visit the job sites where subcontractors are working look for these things:

1. The attitude and expertise of the crews. Do they work diligently with the positive assured movements of experienced craftsmen?

2. Is their work neat, smooth, straight so as to show good workmanship?

3. Is the finished product as completely satisfactory as you would want in your home?

Consider the contractor's personality. Is he knowledgeable in his trade? Is he frank and straightforward in his comments and opinions? Is he prompt in meeting his appointments with you? Is he quick to return your phone calls? Does he have a personal reputation for being cooperative, reliable and a man of integrity?

When interviewing and evaluating subcontractors, bear in mind that you will be *relying upon their knowledge and experience* in their own fields. You will have to depend upon them to be able to go ahead and do a good job without guidance from you or anyone else. *They must be experts* in their trades and fully responsible for their own activities.

Accumulating reference information

Keep written records of the subcontractors as you contact them. Note your impressions and other people's remarks on these records as well as all other pertinent information. Do not trust your memory to keep all the details accumulated in this search for the right subcontractors. (See sample reference card later in the book.) Later when you have received bids and are evaluating the subcontractors, you will find the information on these cards very helpful in determining which ones should be awarded the contracts. The few weeks you spend in this effort is time well spent, which will be evident later as actual construction progresses.

Also, by this time you will have acquired considerable knowledge of the residential construction business, all of which will aid you in the tasks and decisions ahead. Your familiarity with the language will be of great value, also, in your interview with loan company officers. Your ability to talk about the construction business will help remove their reluctance to loan to an owner-builder.

Obtaining bids

Review the information you have obtained on subcontractors and select those you believe will be most suitable for bidding on your various jobs. Remember to select three for each major classification whenever possible. For your own convenience you may want to avoid having too many classifications of subcontractors bidding at the same time. However, if time is important, obtain sufficient sets of plans to have several subcontractors bidding simultaneously.

You may wish to use as a guide the subcontractors listed on the construction cost estimate sheets. Starting at the top, you may have excavating contractors and concrete contractors preparing bids at the same time. Since you will want bids from three subs (subcontractors) in each of these major jobs, you will be working with six at this time.

As soon as the first of these return their bids and their sets of plans, start working with the next classifications. Continue this task until you have bids from all the contractors you will need to complete the construction of your house.

Following are the steps to be taken to obtain bids:

1. Phone the selected subcontractors and set up appointments.

2. Loan each a set of plans and specifications.

3. Discuss the plans and specifications in all the details in which each particular subcontractor will be involved. (Refer to the chapter which gives the scope of activities and responsibilities of subcontractors to help you understand what you should expect from each subcontractor.)

4. Visit the job site with the subcontractor if necessary to clearly convey the conditions that may be important to him (particularly the excavating contractors and concrete contractors).

5. Work out the details of each contract. Discuss the areas of work which interface with other contractors. Be specific in describing the extent of the work to be accomplished by each and the items they are to supply.

6. Stipulate on the contract how changes and extras, if any, are to be charged—usually done on a time-and-material basis. The contract should carry the agreed-upon hourly rate, and the percent of markup (if any) allowed on materials.

7. Let the subcontractors know that they will be paid upon presentation of their bills and that you expect them to consider that advantage when they are pricing their bids.

8. Require the subcontractors to submit written bids (proposals) that are explicit, detailed, signed and dated. Examples of acceptable bid and contract forms are given in the appendices. (The time allowed for you to accept the bid should be at least thirty days.)

9. In most cases, it works to your advantage to let each bidder know that other subcontractors are bidding for the job, too. This avoids the possibility of unnecessarily high bids due to each subcontractor thinking he will get the job anyway, regardless of the price.

    On the other hand, some subcontractors take offense at being asked to bid competitively, and they decline to submit a bid. You may already know the attitudes in your community. If not, it may be necessary for you to make inquiries and explore this problem before you will be able to make the right approach to the contractors in your locality. In general it is not advisable to tell any subcontractor the name of the other subcontractors he is bidding against.

10. Do not get pressured by people, time or weariness into deciding that one bid is enough (unless you personally know your contractors). This is particularly important on the major jobs where large amounts of money are involved. Competitive bidding produces one very desirable result. It saves money.

Some of the minor subcontracts, or those not involved until near completion of the building, may be more convenient to bid after the construction is well under way. This avoids holding up construction while you get the information together. Also, some jobs are easier to bid if the building can be visited, conditions seen and field dimensions taken.

The one problem with this delay is that early in this whole project you will need reasonably accurate cost figures for those unbid jobs in order to compile the cost estimate for the bank or savings and loan company. However, you can get a fair idea of costs by talking to a contractor in the particular business for which you need such information. He can give you an approximate estimate quickly, but he may be reluctant to do so. Some contractors consider such estimates a *no-win* deal. Their thinking is that if they volunteer a rough estimate that is too high they may not get a chance to figure a firm bid. Or, if they give one that is too low, the customer will be unhappy when the firm bid is higher. Nevertheless, you will probably be able to get a rough estimate if you assure the subcontractor that you understand his problem and that you are not asking for a firm bid. Assure him that you will definitely give him the opportunity to give a firm bid when the time comes.

Evaluating the bids and selecting subcontractors

Shortly after you have received the written bids from all the subcontractors in any one classification, you will need to compare bid prices and the specific details of each bid. In determining which subcontractor will be awarded the contract, consider not only the bid price but all the other information you have gathered about each contractor and crew.

The low bid is not always the bid to accept. The advantage of a low bid is soon lost if the contractor fails to perform well, does not show up when expected, is not cooperative, leaves the job with bills unpaid or turns out less-than-satisfactory work.

If there is a considerable difference between the high and low bids, it may be to your best interest to find out why. Again discuss the job with the bidders. Do not tip your hand by discussing other subcontractor's bid prices. Simply inquire as to how they arrived at their estimate without letting them know whether it was high or low. Be sure that they understand fully what you expect them to do to fulfill their contract satisfactorily.

Do not try to take advantage of an extremely low bid without discussing the scope of the job with the bidding subcontractor. Be sure that he can deliver a good quality and complete job for the price he has quoted. You will want to analyze the reasons why he can do the job for so much less. Are his reasons valid? Does he actually have a better way to do the job for less? If not, he may be expecting to make up for his low bid price by adding expensive extras later. Some contractors make a practice of looking for minor errors in the plans so that they can correct them later as an expensive extra, or change, to the contract. They will bid low intentionally, expecting to charge excessively for the changes.

However, most contractors try to deal honestly and will call errors to your attention before they are built into the job, thereby avoiding the expense of rework. If there is an error in the plans and the contractor has built according to the plan, the correction will be at your expense. On the other hand, mistakes made by the contractor's crew are his to correct. Frequently a mistake is not found until later, when another craft discovers that something will not fit. Be alert—a mistake that is found before additional work is done around it is more easily corrected. (More about your inspection activities in Step 8.)

The bid forms (proposals) most generally used by subcontractors are also the contract. When the completed bids are returned to you they need only your signature to make them binding. Before you sign be sure that the written-in part of the contract is detailed and explicit. Check to be sure that it covers all activities, labor, materials, appliances, fixtures and all other items that should be specifically described so that both parties to the contract know exactly what is expected.

Notice on the bid forms the paragraph in small print that binds the subcontractor to provide materials that are to specifications and workmanship that meets good standard practices. The subcontractor is liable for any substandard material or workmanship and must do all rework that is necessary to meet the standards at his own expense. Be sure that your plans and specifications properly call out materials. When the subcontractors are working the job require them to use the right materials and meet standard practices in their work performance. The building inspectors will support you in this. In fact, they will "red tag" any substandard material or workmanship. Also, the law is on your side if you have to go that far in order to get proper performance.

After carefully evaluating the factors involved, select subcontractors for each classification that you believe can best fulfill the contracts at the most reasonable prices. Sign their contracts and notify them. Thank you notes should be sent to the subcontractors that submitted bids but did not receive contracts. They will appreciate the note and your thoughtfulness in letting them know. No one likes to be left in the position of not knowing whether or not they got the job. Keep the note brief. Do not say who received the contract, why you selected the contractor you did, or give the amount of the winning contract. It is only natural for all contractors to believe that they are the best and have the best crews. The only reason they will accept gracefully for not having won the contract is price. That may not have been the entire reason for your choice. Avoid the details rather than offend the loser.

Since lumber is an expensive item, you may be tempted to shop around and buy your own lumber. Perhaps you know a lumber yard where you can get a discount. Also, you may be reluctant to have the framing contractor supply the lumber because you expect that he will add a percentage to the cost of the lumber when he is figuring your bid. Both of these reasons may be valid to some extent, but they do not include all aspects of the problem.

It is recommended that you *require* the framing contractor to include in his bid the costs of all the lumber and other supplies he will need. There are several reasons for this.

1. The contractor should be totally responsible for ordering and receiving the right sizes and quantities of his materials and for getting them on the job at the right time. If you get involved here you will be the fall guy

whenever lumber gets misused or shortages occur and the craftsmen waste time waiting for the right material.

2. The contractor will require his men to make the best use of the material if he is paying for it. On the other hand, if you are paying for the lumber, the contractor will only be interested in saving his labor costs, at the expense of wasted lumber.

3. When bidding competitively it is doubtful that the contractor will mark up the price of the material to exceed the discount that he can obtain from his supplier. And his discount most probably will exceed anything you may be able to obtain.

4. By having the contractor accept this responsibility, you avoid spending your time and energy in an effort that most likely will not produce any worthwhile savings for you.

STEP 8

Construction Schedule

A construction schedule provides assistance for planning, organizing and directing construction activities. This brief discussion and the accompanying outline serve as a preface to the longer description of the construction activities schedule presented in chronological form in Step 9. The purpose of the construction schedule is not so much to tie down dates or time allowances, as it is to provide a method to coordinate the activities of the contractors and others involved in the construction of your house.

One of your prime duties as the owner-builder contractor is to organize and direct the activities. This will require that you make the phone calls to get the right people on the job at the right time. It will also be necessary for you to follow up and see that they arrive at the job site as scheduled. You should follow the work being done and constantly be alert to which other subcontractors should be notified of the progress being made. They should be notified in advance so that they will be prepared to get on the job when you need them. The subcontractors that are working on the job will be able to tell you when they expect to complete a given phase of the work that will require or permit other crafts to come on the job.

It is important to coordinate the activities of the various subcontractors so that each gets the opportunity to get his work done *when it can best be done*. For example: After the foundation is poured, the rough framing crew will be installing the floor joists. Be sure that the plumber has his under-the-floor rough plumbing installed before the subfloor is laid on the joists. Any work that has to be done in the crawl space after the flooring has been laid is much more difficult to do and more expensive.

One of your tasks during the construction period is the frequent examination of the completed construction work, not just the casual observation of the crews at work, but close and critical checking of details, dimensions and positions of: walls, windows and doors; toilet, tub and other rough plumbing stub-out locations; electrical outlets and switch locations; airconditioning and exhaust duct and diffuser locations; other items that you will recognize as important as you watch the progress of the building construction.

A good time to do the checking is after the crews have left for the day when you can check and measure without distractions. Take a tape measure, carpenter's level and a set of the floor plans and be a topnotch inspector. You can avoid more complicated problems by having minor mistakes corrected early.

A good general contractor, who has established contacts with suppliers and subcontractors, can complete the construction of an average size, custom-built residence in about four months, providing he has good weather and no unusual major delays. However, a one-time or first-time owner-builder will probably find the following 23-week schedule more realistic in the overall time span. The weekly schedule as shown is tentative, of course, and may be considered optimal as no unexpected long delays have been built into it. You may find your job ahead of schedule in some stages and behind in others. Do not be disturbed by that. The important thing to remember is to keep each operation as smooth, trouble free and economical as possible.

There are time variables that may apply to your specific circumstance. Conditions may require you to expect a longer construction period: weather conditions, remote location of your property, difficult access to the building site, rough and rocky terrain, no power or water immediately available, or a temporary scarcity of any of the critical materials. All such difficulties should be considered when you are planning your construction schedule if they apply to your situation.

The construction schedule is outlined in its briefest form. The activities that are involved in that schedule are given in the following chapter (Step 9).

CHRONOLOGICAL CONSTRUCTION OUTLINE

Week 1
- Grading; excavating. Temporary water and electrical hookups.

Weeks 2, 3
- Foundation and basement forms; concrete pouring: form stripping.
- Rough plumbing; sewer connection; water lines.
- Subfloor airconditioning ductwork.

Weeks 4, 5, 6
- Framing construction (rough carpentry); trusses.
- Roofing; soffits, fascia, skylights, power vents.

Weeks 7, 8, 9
- Airconditioning duct work.
- Rough plumbing; tubs, showers.
- Electrical wiring; service head; circuit-breaker panel.
- Insulation.
- Exterior sheathing; windows.

Weeks 10, 11, 12
- Drywall installation; texturing, acoustical ceilings.
- Exterior wall coverings; stucco; masonry.

Weeks 13, 14, 15, 16
- Finish carpentry; exterior and interior doors, mouldings, stairs.
- Cabinets; kitchen, bathroom, wardrobes; closets.
- Garage door.
- Ceramic tile work; kitchen, bathrooms, foyer floor.
- Finish grading.
- Concrete driveway, sidewalks, patios, steps, planters, walls.

Weeks 17, 18, 19, 20
- Painting and papering.
- Finish electrical—switches; outlets; light fixtures.
- Finish plumbing—toilets; sinks; faucets. Water heaters; softener.
- Finish airconditioning—condenser; forced air unit; diffusers.
- Finish glass—mirrors, shower doors.
- Lighted ceilings—kitchen hung ceiling; bathroom lighted soffits.
- Carpets and vinyl floorings.
- Drapes; shades; shutters.
- General cleanup.

Weeks 21, 22, 23
- Landscaping.
- Automatic sprinkling systems.
- Fencing.

STEP 9

Construction

At long last the great day will arrive when you can actually begin construction. The following pages take you step by step through the daily activities that you must initiate, direct, coordinate and supervise. You should require of your subcontractors conformance to building codes, regulations, insurance requirements and good construction practices.

Prearrangements

Prior to the actual ground breaking you will have:

1. Arranged for your construction loan;

2. Obtained building permits;

3. Had your lot surveyed, if necessary, to be sure of its boundaries and that the lot you are preparing to build on is, in fact, the lot you purchased;

4. Signed contracts for the first stages of construction;

5. Completed arrangements with the utility companies;

6. Given the utility companies 48 hours notice that you will be excavating on your lot and that you want all underground utility lines located and marked.

Your daily activities as the owner-builder contractor and all the activities of the various subcontractors during the construction period are detailed in the following activity schedule which is broken down into weekly segments. Subcontractors who will be actively involved during these weeks are listed at the beginning of each segment.

Daily activities:

WEEK 1

Excavating • Concrete • Plumber • Electrical

Arrange for a temporary electric power meter to be installed at the job site. Phone your electrical contractor and he will install a post with a circuit-breaker box and outlets on it. He will notify the electric power company to install a meter and hook up the power lines. Check with him to be sure he notifies the power company.

Arrange for a temporary water supply. Phone your plumber contractor and he will arrange for the installation of a meter and hose bib. In some communities you will call the water company and they will install the meter and a hose bib.

Call your concrete contractor and your excavating contractor. Arrange to meet them at the job site to mark out the actual size and position of the house on the lot. Discuss the finish-floor level of the house, finish grade levels and setbacks. (This information should be shown on the plans, but discuss it on the site with these contractors.)

Excavating can begin as soon as the utility companies have located and marked the location of all underground lines. Be sure there are good communications between the utility company people and the excavating contractor's people. You do not want the backhoe digging up a gas main or striking a high voltage power line. In fact, even the telephone company can get quite unhappy if you tear up their lines.

Phone the portable toilet rental company and have them deliver a toilet to the job site.

After rough grading is done, one of the first excavating jobs is to locate the sewer and provide access for the plumber to make the sewer connection. Permits may be required for this and inspections made. Be sure that either you or your plumber make arrangements a day in advance for the inspection.

WEEKS 2, 3

Excavating • Concrete • Plumbing • Airconditioning

Excavating should be completed and forms for the foundation begun. As work progresses, resolve problems that may arise, such as determining the proper height of the foundation so that the main floor is the right height above the street.

Check the dimensions of the forms to be sure they agree with the dimensions shown on the plans. Ask the contractor about any dimensions that may appear to be wrong. Even contractors make mistakes sometimes.

Remember to call for inspection before any concrete is poured in footings or forms. Arrange with the concrete contractor which of you will make the phone call to the inspector. If a definite arrangement is not made, each of you may expect the other to make the phone call to get an inspector, and neither do it. You may lose valuable time waiting for the inspector, or worse yet, have concrete delivered before the inspector has come to make the inspection. As the various contractors come on the job, be sure to have definite understandings with each regarding who will call for inspections. Not all stages of construction are inspected. The number of inspections and what requires an inspection varies greatly in the various areas of the country. Most building permits will indicate when your construction must be inspected.

Be sure the plumbers get the opportunity to run sewer lines and other rough plumbing that must go in before the concrete is poured. Subfloor heating and airconditioning ducts must also be installed before the concrete is poured.

Keep the framing contractor informed of the progress being made. He will need to get his material on order. As the foundation work progresses, discuss scheduling with the concrete contractor and get his opinion as to when he will have the foundation completed and ready for the carpenters. Then let the framing contractor (rough carpentry) know when you expect him to begin work.

Under some loan arrangements you will be able to make your first draw upon completion of the foundation. You will have already accumulated a few bills that must be paid.

WEEKS 4, 5, 6

Framing • Roofing • Trusses

After the concrete crew has completed the foundation or concrete slab floor, stripped the forms, and backfilled against the basement walls, the rough carpentry crew will begin the framing construction. This work goes fast, and they will make good progress in the first week or two. The house you have visualized suddenly becomes real.

You should keep in almost daily contact with the framing contractor and check the job frequently. Check actual construction against the plans and question anything that appears to be wrong. Check wall locations to the plan and have any errors corrected. Sight the walls to be sure they are straight, and plumb the walls with a carpenter's level.

After the exterior insulating sheathing is installed, the window rough openings can give you a fair idea as to the adequacy of the light. If there must be any changes in the size or location of any windows, now is the time they should be corrected before interior or exterior wall coverings are applied. Avoid changes if possible as they are expensive. If a change in the framing is necessary, it can be done at this time at the least expense.

Do not assume the roll of boss to the workmen. They report to, and are responsible to, the subcontractor or his foreman, not to you. Take your problems or suggestions to the subcontractor or his foreman.

Early in this period notify the following subcontractors that the rough framing has begun so that they can make preparations and have a tentative date to work into their schedules: roofing contractor, airconditioning, electrical, insulation, glass and glazing, plumbing. Later, as the framing progresses, you should ask the framing subcontractor when he expects his work to be far enough along for each of the above contractors to have their crews come on the job. Report the progress to these subcontractors and give them more definite start dates.

Windows and doors should be on order by this time. If these are included in your carpentry contract, the subcontractor will take the responsibility for getting the order in. If not, you will want to order these as early as six weeks prior to installation. Check with your supplier to determine the lead time required. Take a set of prints to the supplier and discuss all details to insure that the items you order are correctly and fully described.

If possible, arrange to be at the job site whenever an inspection is to be made. If you cannot be there, be sure that the contractor is there who is most involved in the construction being inspected. If the inspector finds corrections that must be made, require the contractor involved to make the corrections at once in order to avoid delays that will disrupt construction schedules already established with other crafts and subcontractors.

After the stud walls and roof rafters (or trusses) are in place, you should give the following contractors advanced notice so that they can get your job tentatively on their schedules and make appropriate preparations. Later, you will keep them updated as to the progress being made and, at the earliest reasonable time, give them a definite start date: drywall (or plaster) contractor, masonry contractor, stucco contractor, cabinetmaker, finish carpentry, sheet metal.

Cabinetmakers and others will visit the job site to take actual dimensions (field dimensions) from the structure as built in order to be sure that whatever they build or supply from their own shops will fit. Whenever possible, be on hand to answer questions and help resolve problems whenever the contractor or his field men are taking measurements and looking over the job. Be sure they know what you want and how you want it. Communicate well and avoid errors and rework. Remember that most house plans need on-site interpretation and implementing decisions. These decisions should be yours, after considering all the suggestions and alternatives.

Clean up the area. Throughout the entire construction period you will want to maintain clean work areas. This will reduce the possibility of accidents, increase productivity, and even induce better quality workmanship. Subcontractors have a responsibility to remove their own rubbish, nevertheless, the area will will not remain clean unless you supplement their efforts with definite cleanup times and your own help.

When framing is complete and the roofing on, you will be able to make another draw from the loan company (if you are using that loan arrangement).

WEEKS 7, 8, 9

Airconditioning • Plumbing • Electrical • Roofing • Insulation • Glass (windows)

As soon as most of the interior rough framing has been done, heating and airconditioning ductwork can be installed. It should be scheduled in before electrical or plumbing as the routing of the ducts is less flexible than either plumbing or wiring. These latter two craftsmen can run their lines around the airconditioning ducts. You should get these three subcontractors together and resolve interference problems before they are built in.

The plumbers should run their lines in next as the electricians have the most flexibility. Also, electrical wiring is more easily damaged by other workers so should be kept out of the way until the plumbers have run their lines. These three crews (airconditioning, plumbing and electrical) should have no great problems working the house at the same time providing they coordinate and cooperate well.

The electricians should run in the TV lines. In most areas the phone company will install lines. Phone and make arrangements.

Working closely with the framing contractor, get the roofing laid at the earliest possible time. If the fascia and soffits are sheet metal and are to be installed by a separate contractor (sheet metal contractor), be sure you coordinate carefully between the three contractors (framing, roofing and sheet metal). Get their cooperation so that each does his work at the right time and without any crew being required to come back later to complete their job. Windows can and should be installed during this time. The framing contractor will have installed sheathing panels on the exterior walls.

After the electricians, plumbers and phone company are through with their roughin of wiring and plumbing, the insulation contractor can send his crews in. In order to protect the insulation, you will want the drywall crews to go to work as soon as possible after the insulation is in and the required inspections are made. Be sure to notify the drywall contractor far enough in advance so that he will have his crews on the job when needed.

Inspections will be necessary during this time. Keep good communications going with the crafts to be sure Inspectors are notified in time to avoid any delays.

As construction progresses during this period, you will want to call the following subcontractors again as soon as you will be able to give them quite definite starting dates. Never wait until the last minute to let a subcontractor know your job is ready for him. It is far better to call a couple weeks ahead giving him construction progress reports and tentative starting dates. Later call him again when you can give him a definite date: masonry contractor, cabinetmaker, stucco contractor, finish carpenter.

It is a good idea to keep written records of your phone calls to the subcontractors. (Use the back of the subcontractor's file cards—see Appendix C.) Be sure to note when you called, who you talked to, what dates were set and any problems that may be evident. You may find that it is difficult to get the subcontractors on the phone as they frequently are out pursuing the activities of their business. Try to find out when they can most easily be reached by phone and note that on your record card for reference.

During the construction process, you will need to find time to see and firm up decisions on such items as the following:

- Kitchen and bathroom cabinets—colors, style, quality;
- Front entry door and hardware;
- Brick, stone and siding—type, colors;
- Plumbing fixtures—color, style, size, make, model;
- Paint colors and wall papers; paneling;
- Ceramic tile—colors, styles;
- Foyer and Entry flooring—tile, brick, vinyl, parquet;
- Appliances—kitchen, laundry room;
- Bathroom heat and vent fixtures;
- Kitchen vent hood;
- Light fixtures;

- Carpets, vinyl flooring;

- Drapes, curtains, shades, shutters.

WEEKS 10, 11, 12, 13

Drywall • Stucco • Masonry • Finish Carpenter • Cabinetmakers • Painter

After the building inspector has signed off the framing construction, rough electrical and plumbing, the drywall contractor can put his crew to work on the interior. They will install the drywall, tape and smooth putty the joints, texture the walls and spray acoustic materials on the ceilings. They will need very little input from you except to know what texture you prefer and in what areas you will want a smooth finish. The areas to be wallpapered should be left smooth.

During this time the masonry, exterior siding and/or stucco work can be done. The masons will need to know such details as the color of the grout you prefer. The bond pattern of the brick should be shown on the plans by the architect. Be sure the brick mason lays the brick in the pattern the designer specified. Small details do make a difference in the finished appearance. The stucco contractor will need to know what color you prefer for the finish coat.

Early in this period you should discuss with the finish carpenter the materials he will be ordering for the job. You should see the various styles of moldings that are available and decide which ones are to be used. Discuss the details of items such as the cabinets, closets, wardrobes, stairs: number and location of shelves and clothes poles in wardrobes; style and type of doors; type and color of hinges and handles; all other details that you will want to determine to suit your own preferences.

The finish carpenters can go to work as soon as the drywall crews have completed their work and cleaned up their work areas. They will hang doors; install door casings, baseboards and other moldings; complete linen closets, wardrobes, stairways and all other woodworking details that are not part of the cabinetmaker's contract. Near the end of this period the cabinetmakers should be able to bring in their shop-built cabinets and install them.

If your building has a wood exterior that will require staining, painting or varnishing, the painter should be notified early and required to apply the protective finish as soon as the construction process will permit.

When you are working out the contracts you should be specific in stating who will install the cabinets. Generally it is best for the cabinetmakers to install their own cabinets. This places the full responsibility for well built and good fitting cabinets on one contractor. If you purchase factory-built cabinets, you should specify in the finish carpenter's contract that he will install these cabinets.

During this time you will be able to give advance notice to the following: ceramic tile contractor, finish grading contractor, finish concrete contractor.

WEEKS 14, 15, 16
Finish Carpenter • Cabinetmaker • Ceramic Tile • Finish Grading • Finish Concrete

The finish carpenters and cabinetmakers will continue their work. Schedule the ceramic tile subcontractor's crew to come in when the cabinetmakers have completed their installations in the kitchen and bathrooms. Before this time you will have made your decisions on color, size and type of tile to be used. The tile contract may also include floors for the bathrooms, entry, foyer, shower walls and tub surrounds. Generally these crews can work right through from start to finish without interruption for other crafts.

During this period the exterior of the house should be completed by the masons and stucco crews. Finish grading around the house can then be done. Concrete driveways, sidewalks, steps, patios and garden walls can be done by the finish concrete contractor's crews.

Be sure to check local requirements regarding permits and inspections that may be required during the activities of this period. For instance, most cities require a permit to cut the city curb for a driveway.

The painting contractor should be notified during this time. The finish carpenters will be able to tell you in advance when the job will be ready for the painter. Also, complete your arrangements for carpets and draperies.

WEEKS 17, 18, 19, 20
Painting • Electrical • Plumbing • Airconditioning • Carpets • Drapes

Interior and exterior painting, wall papering, and paneling should be completed the first part of this period. A neutral color (mostly a creamy white) is used for interior walls in most homes today, as it provides the most suitable background for furniture and a wide variety of colors in carpets. This also simplifies the painter's job, as getting just the right tint or shade of color to please a customer is sometimes quite difficult. However, if you have selected special colors for some areas, be sure to take the time to be on hand when your painter begins his work using those colors. After a small area has been painted you may find that the color is not satisfactory. It is much better to discover a mistake before a whole room has been completed.

As soon as the painter can give you a date when he will complete his work, notify the electrical, plumbing and airconditioning contractors. They will need to schedule their finish crews in to complete their work. Also the carpet and draperies suppliers should be notified of the dates when they will be expected. Allow one week for the electricians, airconditioning and plumbers to complete their finish work before the carpets can be laid.

The electricians will come back to hang light fixtures, install switches and outlets, check out their circuits and complete their work. The plumbers will set toilets, connect up sinks, hot water tanks, water softeners and complete their work. The airconditioning men will install diffusers, hook up the condensing unit, air-handling unit, charge the system with freon and check it out. Near the end of this period the carpets, vinyl floor coverings, drapes and window blinds may be installed.

If you desire to have landscaping done before you move in, complete your arrangements for lawn sprinkling systems, landscaping and fencing and give these subcontractors starting dates for their work.

WEEKS 21, 22, 23

Fencing • Lawn Sprinkler System • Landscaping

These optional contractor activities are not necessarily a part of the construction of your house. Filing a completion notice and obtaining an occupancy permit is not dependent upon the completion of the landscaping of the lot.

However, it is necessary, upon completion of the house, to do a very thorough cleanup of the premises. Remove all rubbish and present a neat finished product by taking care of such minor details as touching up the finish grading around sidewalks, driveway, patios and steps. Expect an inspection to be made before your housekeeping deposit will be returned. (Many areas require a deposit of a few hundred dollars before construction begins which is held as a guarantee that you will keep the area reasonably clean at all times. If you fail to keep construction debris cleaned up, others will be hired to clean it up and will be paid out of the deposit.)

Call for the final inspection and obtain the building occupancy permit. Make out checks for all final payments and take any steps necessary to assure that no cause exists for any mechanic's liens to be filed against the property. See Appendix E for waiver of liens instructions. Make arrangements with your bank, or loan company, to close out the construction loan and assume the long-term mortgage loan.

Move in and enjoy your new home. You will be pleased with it and proud of what you have accomplished.

CONCLUSION

This book deals with the details of everyday activities, so that a person without a great deal of home construction knowledge can, nevertheless, successfully organize and supervise others who are the construction specialists. Taken as a whole, such a construction project has to be recognized as quite involved and extensive. It is not my intention to imply otherwise. However, it is an obtainable objective when approached in the manner and with the methods described in this book.

It is prudent to consider both the negative aspects as well as the advantages. You may want to consider the following aspects as they may be considered difficult and demanding:

- You will be actively involved in this project for a period of approximately six to eight months. Not necessarily full time, but certainly you should expect it to dominate your mind and require considerable attention.

- You will be challenged to learn and become knowledgeable in what may be new areas. You will need this information in order to make right decisions.

- It will be necessary for you to have the ability to plan, organize, communicate and implement actions.

- It will not be necessary for you to be able to do any of the many specialized construction jobs. You need only to know how to get others to do them. It will be necessary for you to rely upon the expertise, knowledge and experience of others. *Select the best you can find.*

In summary then, the purpose of this book is to give you, in the most concise and systematic way possible, the information you will need to successfully plan, organize, communicate, and obtain the activities necessary to construct your new home. Building your own home can be not only financially advantageous, but interesting, challenging and a happy experience. Anticipating each day's activities and looking forward to the completion of a beautiful house is pleasant and rewarding when you are contributing your own time and talent.

Appendix A

Insurance

What and why

As an owner-builder your cash outlay for insurance will be minimal compared to that required for fulltime contractors. Nevertheless, you need to be aware of insurance requirements and how insurance can benefit you.

There are several types of insurance involved in your project. Some you will only be aware of, others you will need to know to be sure that they are in force.

Title insurance

This very common insurance is obtained for you almost automatically when you purchase your lot and again at the time you place the construction loan and long-term mortgage upon your property. You will pay a nominal fee for this benefit at the time of the transactions.

The purpose of the title insurance policy is to guarantee that the ownership of the property is as stated in the deed. Essentially the policy guarantees that the title to the property is free and clear of encumbrances or liens. If it proves not to be so, you have recourse against the title insurance company.

Liability insurance

Most people already carry some type of liability insurance. Frequently this is in conjunction with their existing real property, homeowner's or renter's insurance, or their auto insurance. However, you will want to discuss your coverage with your insurance agent to be sure that you are insured against liability to the public for injury at the construction site.

Builder's risk policy

This is a short-term policy that will cover damage to the property that may occur during construction. Generally the policy covers loss due to fire or windstorm and such extended coverage as may be listed. Frequently this short-term policy is written as a rider on the long-term fire insurance policy that you will take out to cover the new house.

If the builder's risk policy and the homeowner's fire insurance policy are separate, they should be written by the same insurance company to avoid disputes that may arise between two companies each disclaiming responsibility for payment when a specific incident occurs.

Workman's compensation insurance

This is the insurance you will be most concerned with during the life of your construction project. Most states have laws requiring employers to carry workman's compensation insurance. This insurance guarantees compensation to workmen that may be injured on the job or to his estate if he is killed on the job.

In your capacity as owner-builder contractor you may subcontract all work done on your project. In that case you will not have any employees of your own and, technically, you would not need to obtain a workman's compensation insurance policy. The subcontractors will be responsible for the insurance on their employees. You will want proof that the subcontractor's employees are, in fact, covered by insurance. More about that later.

As mentioned earlier in this book, the owner-builder has several options and may choose the construction arrangements that best suit his particular circumstances. If you choose to let contracts only for the major work classifications and expect to employ individuals to do the minor, or selected jobs, then you may be required by law, in most states, to cover these individuals with compensation insurance.

If not actually required by law in your state, you may be well advised to get the coverage anyway as the common practice throughout this country today is to place the responsibility upon the property owner for compensation to any workman injured while working on the property. Large amounts of money may be involved in case of injury or death.

Experience suggests that the following are reasonable guidelines for handling your responsibilities regarding workman's compensation insurance. However, it is not implied that these suggestions are legal interpretations of the insurance laws as might be obtained from a lawyer or insurance specialists.

1. Require all subcontractors to have workman's compensation insurance in force while their men are working your job. Verification is advisable. Have each subcontractor notify his insurance company to send you a

certificate that will show that the insurance is in force and give the names of the employees that are covered. This verification should be in your hands before the subcontractor's crews start work.

2. Take out a blanket policy to cover anyone that might be working the project but who, for one reason or another, might not be covered by other insurance. Workmen not covered by other insurance could include such as: A day laborer who might work for only a day or two as a cleanup man. A new workman for one of your subcontractors who has not been included on his insured list. The employee of a minor subcontractor from whom you failed to get proof of workman's compensation insurance. If an accident happens to one of his employees you may find that the contractor was not carrying workman's compensation insurance. However, you will be protected by your blanket policy.

Owner-builder as employer

This subject is included here under the general heading of insurance simply because the governmental obligations a person acquires, if he qualifies as an employer, are primarily related to insurance and compensation in one form or another. This is general information and should not be considered legal interpretations of the numerous laws pertaining to employers as might be obtained from a lawyer or representative of the government.

First a definition of "employer" and then some words of caution. In many states, if you employ or otherwise engage any person (other than a member of your immediate family) to perform any task on your property, or project, you may be an employer, providing the total cost of the project exceeds $200. Persons representing themselves as contractors or subcontractors must be licensed as such, otherwise they are considered your employees. Unlicensed persons cannot legally enter into a work contract with you.

Consider the hazards, responsibilities and extra expense that many states and the federal government place upon employers. As an employer you will be required to comply with the following: Register with the state and federal governments as an employer. Provide for state and federal income tax withholding, federal social security taxes, workman's compensation insurance, disability insurance costs, unemployment compensation contributions, preparation and maintenance of accurate accounting records of all employee related transactions.

It is recommended that you use fully qualified, properly insured, licensed subcontractors to the fullest extent possible when building your home. Avoid placing yourself in the position of an employer.

Appendix B

Building Permits

Working with inspectors

The issuing of building permits and requiring conformance to building codes and regulations is a common practice throughout most of the United States and Canada whether in large cities or rural areas. The extent and complexity of the regulations and their implementing organizations varies greatly from the elaborate and rigidly controlled large city departments of health and safety to simple regulation enforcement by a county building inspector in rural areas.

As the owner-builder you will want all of your construction to conform to high-standard building codes, regardless of the sometimes minimal requirements of your local building regulations. Most building codes are based on good building construction practices and are guidelines to ensure the home owner a well constructed house.

It is also in your best interest to make every effort to cooperate with your inspector and comply with the building department requirements. Be considerate of the demands upon their time. Build a friendly, cooperative attitude between yourself and the inspectors. Listen to their advice, follow their suggestions and instructions. Always notify them far enough in advance to obtain their inspections at the right time. Never think that you can avoid complying with their rules and regulations, or that you can change the system by your objections.

How to apply for building permits

Your first step is to find out what the requirements are in your area and how to comply with them. If you propose to build in a large, heavily populated city or county area, you will find the requirements extensive and the procedures somewhat complex. They will have written instructions for you to follow and many people to talk to.

If you are fortunate enough to be building in a smaller city or county area you will most probably find the requirements are minimal and the compliance simple. Since the requirements and procedures vary greatly between large cities and small town and county areas, they will be dealt with separately.

Small cities and counties

In the smaller cities and rural areas, you will go to the city hall or county building and obtain from the building department (or similarly named office) written or verbal information on the local building requirements and procedures.

You will need to know such as the following:

- What information must be shown on the house plans;
- Number of copies of the plans they will need;
- What stages of construction must be inspected;
- How to request inspections (Who do you contact, when and how.);
- What other agencies, if any, must be notified and permission obtained from them to build, grade or whatever;
- The customary arrangements in your area regarding separate permits for electrical, plumbing and sewers;
- In most areas an overall building permit is issued to the owner-builder or general contractor, and certain subcontractors are required to obtain their own permits for their specific trade. The most common specialized permits required are for electrical and plumbing;
- The cost of the permit is usually based upon the square footage of the building to be constructed.

Large cities and heavily populated counties

In these areas the procedures become more complex and may involve more than one agency of government. To obtain a building permit you may be required to proceed somewhat as follows:

1. Discuss requirements, prior to preparing the house plans, with the zoning administration and public information section of the department of building and safety. (This is the most commonly used title, however some of the departments that are trying to broaden the scope of their jurisdictions have changed their names to such as "environmental management agency". Ask for the building department and you will most probably be pointed in the right direction.)

The zoning administration and public information section will provide you with written information and instructions. They will discuss specific details with you regarding your property, such as:

- Zoning—what you may build in the zone where your property is located;
- The proposed use of the building;
- Setback requirements (distance buildings must be from your property lines);
- Building height limitations;
- Parking and garage requirements;
- Legal building site requirements;
- Access and easement questions;
- Special review requirements of current planning, zoning and development committees.

2. See the environmental management agency and local conservation commission (if any in your community). Discuss your project and determine if any action is required of you to comply with their regulations.

3. Visit the public service counter of the engineering section of the department of building and safety. The engineering section should provide you with pamphlets that give specific information on the construction methods, procedures and regulations to meet the local construction codes.

4. Having accumulated this information, you can proceed to have your house plans prepared.

5. Submit your plans and specifications (with engineering calculations if required) to the zoning administration. They will check your plans for compliance with the above mentioned zoning and environmental requirements. If satisfactory, they will clear the plans for presentation to the engineering section for a plan check. (Expect a plan check fee.)

    Engineering will thoroughly check your plans and if they are not satisfactory they will return them with the errors and omissions noted. It is your architect's responsibility to make the changes required by the plan check engineers, at his expense.

6. After the plans are approved by engineering plan check, submit them to the excavating and grading section to determine if a grading permit is required. If required, have grading plans prepared. Submit copies, usually three, to excavating and grading section for plan check. (Again there

will be a fee.) After the grading plans are approved a grading permit will be issued. (Another fee for the permit to grade.) In some areas the rough grading is required to be done (per the approved grading plans) before the building permit will be issued. This restraint is usually found only in very hilly or otherwise difficult building areas.

7. Finally a building permit will be issued upon payment of the permit fees plus, sometimes, a special service fee for parks, etc. One set of the structural plans will be stamped "approved" and an inspector's record card will be issued to you. Both of these items are to be kept available on the project site. You should be handed a sheet of instructions entitled "When to call for inspections." If not, be sure to request one.

    Following is an example of typical inspection instructions for a large city or heavily populated county.

CENTRAL OFFICE
400 Civic Center Dr. West
Santa Ana, Ca 92701
714/ 834-2630
714/ 834-2631

REGIONAL OFFICE
26052 Getty Dr.
Laguna Niguel, Ca 92677
714/ 831-7880
714/ 831-7881

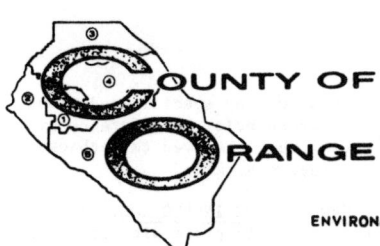

County of Orange

ENVIRONMENTAL MANAGEMENT AGENCY
REGULATION

WHEN TO CALL FOR INSPECTIONS

INSPECTION REQUESTS MUST BE MADE BY 4:00 P.M. IN ORDER TO HAVE INSPECTIONS THE FOLLOWING DAY. PLEASE NOTE THAT YOUR INSPECTION REQUEST MAY BE REFERRED TO A TAPE RECORDING DEVICE WHICH WILL ALLOW YOU THE CONVENIENCE OF CALLING FOR INSPECTIONS AT ANY HOUR, 24 HOURS A DAY. PLEASE SPEAK CLEARLY IN THE PHONE GIVING THE FOLLOWING INFORMATION: (1) OWNER'S NAME; (2) JOB ADDRESS (SPELL STREET NAME); (3) THE PERMIT NUMBER AS SHOWN AT THE BOTTOM OF YOUR PERMIT, AND (4) THE TYPE OF INSPECTION YOU NEED, AS SELECTED FROM THE LIST BELOW.

1. GRADING INSPECTIONS. Refer to comprehensive list of inspections outlined in the "Required Inspections For Grading" handout, available from Earth Sciences Section.

    a. Pregrading meeting/inspection - Held prior to any grading, brushing, clearing, or grubbing preparatory to grading.

    b. Subsequent inspections - Are required for earthwork excavations and fills, concrete drainage devices, asphalt paving and erosion control facilities.

    c. Rough grading inspection - Is required when all rough grading has been completed. Under a Precise Grading Permit, upon approval of site conditions and required reports and certifications, building permits may be issued.

    d. Final inspection - When all work has been completed, including installation of all drainage structures and other protective devices; and when the as-graded plan, required certifications and reports have been submitted. (See Item No. 12).

        NOTE: Approved temporary sanitary facilities shall be on the job site.

2. FOUNDATION (FOOTING) INSPECTION. When all trenches for footings, piers, etc., are excavated and reinforcement, anchor bolts, etc., are in place, electrical ground electrode is installed.

    NOTE: Property line survey markers shall be exposed and marked with licensed surveyor's or registered engineer's tags. Additional property line stakes shall be placed when deemed necessary by the Building Inspector, such as curved or irregular property lines, steep topography, or any other situation where it is difficult to determine an accurate yard setback measurement. (Note: When applicable, slab elevation blue top stakes shall be in place).

NOTE: Check plans, specifications, and soil reports for any special conditions, clearances, or certifications which may be needed prior to clearance by the Building Inspector. Particular attention must be given to setbacks adjacent to public rights-of-way (roads), easements, etc.

3. **PLUMBING (MECHANICAL AND ELECTRICAL WHEN INSTALLED) GROUND WORK INSPECTION.** After rough plumbing (mechanical and electrical when installed) is in place with trenches open.

4. **PRE-SLAB INSPECTION.** (When not placed monolithically with footing). After all utility work is cleared, trenches are backfilled, all fill adequately compacted and certified where applicable, membrane and reinforcement installed, if required.

   NOTE: Check plans, specifications, and soil reports for conditions and/or certifications which may be required on compaction of utility trenches which occur under the building.

5. **UNDERPINNING INSPECTION.** (On wood floor systems). After all work, prior to installing sub-floor, has been completed, and plumbing ground work and underfloor heating ducts have been inspected and cleared. (See Note at Item No. 8 below if masonry construction is involved).

6. **ROOF DECK AND CHIMNEY CORE GROUTING INSPECTION.** After roof decking (solid or spaced) is applied and flashing and roof jacks are in place or on the job. Chimney reinforcement is inspected prior to grouting of the core.

   NOTE: Metal rafter ties in exposed beam construction must be inspected before roof sheathing is applied.

   NOTE: Wood shingles and/or shakes shall be on job site.

   NOTE: Roof deck shall be cleared of loose material, scraps, equipment, etc., to insure proper inspection.

   NOTE: Cant strips, saddles and flashings shall not be installed until the diaphragm nailing of plywood roof decks are inspected and approved.

7. **ROUGH ELECTRICAL, PLUMBING, AND HEATING.** After all rough work is installed and prior to calling for frame inspection. Bathtub access panels must be grounded out, shower pans installed, filled with water, and water service connected.

   NOTE: Those provisions related to the electrical, plumbing and heating systems, which are necessary to insure the required sound attenuation between adjoining living units, shall be installed.

8. **FRAME INSPECTION.** After framing and roof covering is completed and rough electrical, plumbing and heating inspections have been approved. All plaster grounds and exterior metal base screeds shall be in place. Required felt installed around all shower areas and fireplace must be completed.

   NOTE: On masonry construction, see Section 2415(b) 3 of the Uniform Building Code, or contact the Structural Inspection Section of Quality Control Division on when inspections are required.

   NOTE: Insulation material, as required on the approved plan, shall be on the job site at time of frame inspection.

-3-

9. <u>INSULATION (SOUND/THERMAL) INSPECTION</u>. After all required insulation material has been installed according to the plans and details. Resilient channels, when required to receive drywall, shall be installed.

10. <u>LATH AND DRYWALL INSPECTION</u>. After all lathing and drywall, interior and exterior, is in place, plastering permit has been obtained, and plastering material must be on the job.

11. <u>PLASTER INSPECTION</u>. After the second, or brown coat, has been in place for a period of not less than (7) days.

12. <u>FINAL INSPECTION</u>. After building is complete and ready for occupancy, which includes provisions for lot drainage and grading, and clearances from other regulating County agencies involved with the project have been obtained. The order of called final inspections may be at the builder's convenience, however, please remember that all final inspections must be made and cleared before utilities are released and Certificate of Occupancy issued. This includes any zoning and/or grading final. (See Item 1-c above).

Thank you for your kind cooperation.

DM/sk

Appendix C

Subcontractor's File Cards

File cards (3" x 5" or 4" x 6" sizes) are convenient for recording the information you accumulate on subcontractors. Prepare a card on each when you first contact them recording the information on the front of the card as illustrated below. Your follow-up contacts can be recorded on the back side.

You will be meeting many new people in your search for contractors. Your recorded information will be very helpful, not only for quick reference for phone numbers and names, but also the accumulated information will help you decide which contractors are best qualified.

```
Classification: Excavating
Contractor: D. G. Diggers Co.
   Address: 1234 Main St. Clara
   Phone: 673-3422      Contact: "Dave"
Recommended by: Hilltop Supply;
Anderson Lumber; Dean Smith

Remarks: Good equipment, very busy.
Dave- friendly, business-like.
Communicates well. Prompt replies.
Good credit rating. Well recommended
by others.

                                  Rating "A"
```

Contacts - Phone Calls

Date	Time	Who	Remarks
11/30/80	6 P.M.	Dave	See him Fri. 9 A.M. (12/5) @ equip. yard 2406 S. Main St. Clara
12/4	4 P.M.	wife	Dave will call about 6:30 tonite.
12/4	6:30	Dave	called - meet him 9:30 @ job site Fri. 12-5
12/8	6:30	Dave	When bid? Probably Fri. Eve. He will call.

# Appendix D

Common Construction Terms

architectural control committee   A committee comprised of local property owners who have been selected from the community and given the responsibility to assure compliance with the local protective covenants, reservations, conditions and restrictions. Plans for new construction, alterations, additions, etc. must be approved by the committee prior to commencement of the work. The committee usually collects a modest fee and a performance deposit. The committee operates for the benefit of the community to sustain property values and preserve the beauty and environment of the community. Many localities do not have the benefits of protective covenants and architectural control committees.

backfill   The dirt that is put back to fill an area after concrete work has been completed, such as the dirt that is put in around basement walls or over a septic tank and sewer lines. "Backfill" is also used to describe the *act of putting* the dirt back, i.e., to backfill a trench is to fill it with dirt and tamp it down.

bearing walls   This term is the commonly used short form of "load-bearing walls". As the name implies these walls support the loads of the floors (or ceilings) above them.

bond pattern   Bricks and blocks can be laid up in several different ways creating various patterns in the joints where they are bonded together with mortar. For example: "Running bond" is probably the most common pattern. All the bricks run lengthwise and overlap one-half brick. "Stack bond" is a decorative pattern used mostly as a veneer. All joints are aligned vertically and horizontally.

contingency   An amount of money set aside to meet unexpected or overlooked expenses. Experienced contractors know that every job has its own unexpected situations or problems that generate expenses that were not included in the original cost estimate. They add on to their estimated cost a percentage of the total to cover these contingencies.

draws (also known as *progress payments*)   A fixed percentage of the total amount of the construction loan becomes available to the contractor when he completes a specified segment of the construction. Refer to Step 3 which gives more details regarding this subject.

fascia or *fascia boards*   The trim board on the outer edge of the eaves. Usually made of 2" thick lumber. Recently metal fascia has come into more widespread use as it requires less frequent repainting.

field dimensions   Accurate measurements taken from the house as constructed. (They may differ somewhat from the dimensions shown on the plans.)

field glazed   This term applies to the installation of unframed glass into a built-in window frame in the house.

flashings   Aluminum sheets or galvanized sheet metal used for rain gutters on the roof; or as a means to prevent rain from running in between a masonry chimney and the roof. Also used as a moisture barrier between concrete and wood framing.

foundations   The complete concrete work that supports the building structure. The various parts of the foundation are:

>   *footings*   The lowest part of the foundation. Usually 8" deep and from 12" to 20" wide depending upon soil conditions and local building codes. Footings run continuously around the perimeter of the building and around the outer edges of porches, patios, etc. to support concrete slab floors. Also continuous footings are poured under all bearing walls.
>
>   *stem walls*   They sit on the perimeter footings and extend upward to support the floor and upper structure of the house. Stem walls vary in thickness from 6" to 11" depending upon the nature of the structure they will be supporting. Plans specify stem wall thickness.
>
>   *concrete slab floors*   Poured on top of the stem wall or supported by a ledge formed into the top of the stem wall, slab floors are considered part of the foundation.

general building contractor   An individual, partnership or corporation that is licensed by the state as a builder who may legally contract to build for *other* people. He enters into contracts with specialized contractors (subcontractors) to provide the labor, materials and supervision to perform the construction.

insulation R factors   Insulation provides a resistance to a change in temperature. The amount of *R*esistance that the various materials provide is indicated by R factors. For example: R-11 is the minimum insulation recommended for exterior walls. R-19 does a better job of insulating and is the minimum recommended for ceilings. Many homes are now being built with much higher R values to conserve energy.

interface   An area of responsibility or an activity that is common to two or more crafts or contractors that can be assumed or performed by either. The owner-builder contractor should discuss these areas with the contractors and determine which one can best perform the task. Inform both parties of his decision before the bids are prepared. Interface is also that border area of work where one craft finishes and another starts. For example, the framing carpenter rough frames doorways, the finish carpenter installs the door frames and doors.

loan points   A onetime fee or charge for making the loan. Currently a common practice of banks and savings and loan companies. Each point is 1 percent of the total loan. The number of points charged increases with the scarcity of money to loan and may vary between one lending institution and another.

mechanic's lien   A legal action taken to collect just compensation for labor performed or materials provided for the maintenance, repair, construction or improvement of real property. (*See* Appendix E, Waiver of Lien.)

masonry veneer   A solid brick wall is just that and usually 8″ thick. A brick veneer wall is the usual 2 x 4 stud wall construction with a 4″ brick veneer attached to the exterior face of the wall. A masonry veneer wall provides better insulating qualities than a solid brick or block wall.

native soil   This term is used to identify *undisturbed* natural soil.

owner-builder contractor   An individual who builds for himself. He may legally enter into contracts with specialized subcontractors to provide the labor, material, supervision, etc. to perform the construction. He is *not* required to be licensed. He may *not contract to build for other people,* nor may he build for others except as their employee.

percolation tests A method for determining how fast water will sink into the soil and what volume is required to saturate the soil. Specific data and methods for making the tests have been developed which are used by cities and counties to determine if a septic system or cesspool will perform satisfactorily in a given area.

progress payments See draws.

re-bar Commonly used term to describe reinforcing rod.

soil compaction The wetting and tamping of loose soil or sand to obtain a firm soil. Any soil that has been disturbed (moved) should be wet down and compacted before a concrete slab is poured on it. Preferably, it will be mechanically compacted. Footings should be in native (undisturbed) soil, however, they may be placed in *properly compacted* soil that will test 96 percent or better.

soffits The metal or plywood coverings on the underside of overhanging eaves. They should contain vents that provide ventilation to the attic. The term is also used to describe the closed-in areas above kitchen cabinets and the lighted boxed-in areas over the lavatories in bathrooms.

surrounds Tile or cultured marble that is installed on the deck and walls around a tub or in a shower; the glass enclosure of a shower. Also, sometimes used to describe the brick veneer or other fireproof wall covering behind a stove or heater.

subcontractor A licensed specialized contractor. His license is limited to his specialized trade, such as electrical contractor. He may contract to perform his trade with a general contractor, an owner-builder contractor or any individual who wants work done on his own property. (There is no legal difference between the last two classifications.) In general practice and in the text of this book, the terms "subcontractor", "contractor" and "sub" are frequently interchanged.

tradeoffs The exchange of one item for another or one method for another. The term usually implies an alternate option that may be less desirable but necessary under the circumstances.

sub Slang abbreviation for subcontractor. Also a prefix for an item beneath a similar item as a subfloor.

Appendix E

Cost Control Accounting

Simplified accounting system

A simplified method for recording expected costs (or expenditures) and actual amounts paid out is a great convenience. To maintain financial control, the recording of all expenditures is necessary and should be done frequently enough to avoid the possibility of an expenditure not being recorded. You will be refering to this record frequently to determine how you are doing. It may act as a reminder of the tradeoffs that you will have to arrange to keep your budget in balance.

In order to complete the project with the funds available, overruns must be monitored and actions taken to balance the account by reducing some other expenditures. The following suggested form provides columns for recording the over/under amounts as well as a running balance which shows whether or not you have equalized the over/under expenditures. The column for accumulated total expenditures keeps you informed on the total you have spent to date. You can easily figure how much you have left to complete the project. You may wish to enter the total amount of your estimate at the top of the column for a ready reference.

Footnotes to explain over/under amounts can be helpful (see sample on page 90).

Construction progress draws

The two methods most commonly used are:

1. The loan company releases a percent of the total loan upon the completion of a specified stage of construction, i.e., usually the first draw is for 25 percent. It is available to the contractor upon completion of the foundation; the second draw is available when the framing is completed, etc.

2. The general contractor, or owner-builder, periodically presents his accumulation of bills to the loan company (*see* Builder's Request for Construction Advance). They issue the checks to the various suppliers and subcon-

$65,000

Date	Item	Supplier Contractor	Am't. Paid	Orig. Est.	(over) under	*#	Run. Bal.	Accum. Tot. exp.
6-20-80	FINANCING	SOUTH S&L	1175	1350	175	1.	175	1175
6-21-80	HOUSE PLANS	J.B. JONES	2150	2150	—		—	3325
6-24	PERMITS	BUILD. DEPT.	735	500	⟨235⟩	2.	⟨60⟩	4060
6-24-80	UTILITIES DEPOSITS	ELEC. WATER	275	300	25		⟨35⟩	4335
6-28	EXCAVATING	DIGGER Co.	2400	2400	—		—	6735
7-10-80	CONCRETE WORK	JENSON	8550	8350	⟨200⟩	3.	⟨235⟩	15285

*1. LOAN POINTS WERE LESS THAN EXPECTED.
2. EXCAVATING & GRADING PERMIT REQ'D. + $100 PARK FEE.
3 CONC. STEPS ADDED - AN "EXTRA - MUST FIND "TRADE-OFF."

---

tractors. The checks have a lien waiver imprinted on them. When the contractor endorses the check, he is also signing the lien waiver.

If you operate under the first method, you will be responsible for writing the checks to the suppliers and contractors. Be sure you have them sign lien waivers. Under this method you may find that the amount of the draw does not provide enough cash to cover all the bills that should be met before you receive the next draw. In which case you will be paying bills with your own funds (which you indicated would be available when you applied for the loan). Usually most of your personal funds will be used near the completion of the project. Be sure to keep them in reserve to have them available when needed.

Waiver of lien

Whenever a person enters into a contract with another person or company, it is expected that the contract will benefit both parties—one receives goods and services that he needs, the other receives money for the materials and services he has provided. A subcontractor is expected to fulfill his contractual obligations in a business-like manner and to operate his business in a professional way. This includes paying his employees regularly and his material suppliers promptly.

However, since you have no real control over the contractor's business activities (nor any real way to obtain current information on his daily financial operation), it is advisable to require a waiver of lien from each contractor or supplier whenever you write them a final check. A typical waiver of lien form is illustrated below.

Another way to accomplish this is to obtain a rubber stamp and stamp the back of your checks. The rubber stamp states that by endorsing the check the person thereby waives and releases all right to lien against your property, and, also assumes the responsibility to furnish a waiver of lien from all persons or companies furnishing labor or material who may be his employees or suppliers.

The rubber stamp method is more convenient, easier to implement and less apt to be overlooked or postponed too long. It is not necessary for you to contact the person to get his signature. You can pay your bill by mail knowing that when he endorses your check he is signing the lien waiver.

WAIVER OF LIEN

To_____

I, the undersigned _____
the duly authorized representative of_____
hereby acknowledge the receipt of the sum of $_____paid to me for work performed and/or material supplied, in consideration of which I hereby waive and release all lien or right of lien now existing, or that may hereafter arise for work or labor performed, or material furnished on or before the___day of _____, 19___, for the maintenance, repair or improvement of the following property situated in_____County, State of_____to wit:

_____

And I further agree to furnish a good and sufficient waiver of lien on said premises from every person or persons, company or corporation furnishing labor or materials for said premises, who may be acting under any contract or sales agreement with me.

I hereby certify that the labor and material, or both, receipted for the above was actually performed, or used at the above described property.

Dated_____19__,   _____

The owner-builder should give due consideration to the importance of the mechanic's lien law and take the appropriate steps to avoid the possibility of a lien being placed against his property. Any person furnishing labor, materials, equipment or services can place a lien on your property if he has not been paid within a reasonable time. Such claims are given precedence and become a cloud on the title to your property. This must be cleared before a long-term mortgage can be placed on the property or before the title can be transferred. Clearing the title can be time consuming and costly.

It is important to understand that this law applies not only to people who you have personally dealt with but also to any person *employed by the subcontractors* who have worked on your project. The law also includes those supplying materials or services to your subcontractors. If your subcontractor fails to pay his employees or suppliers, those employees and suppliers have recourse against *your* property through the lien law regardless of the fact that you may have paid the contractor.

Don't panic! The law provides protection for you, too. The "waiver of lien" provides that protection, but *you must use it* in one form or another to get that protection. The three most common methods of obtaining this protection are:

1. Use of waiver of lien forms. (*See* sample.) They may be obtained from stationery stores. Fill in all blank spaces and have the subcontractor, worker or materials supplier sign the waiver whenever you pay your construction bills.

2. By using a rubber stamp. Stamp the waiver-of-lien statements on the back of all checks you use to pay for construction costs. As noted above, when the payee endorses the check he is also signing the lien waiver. (Waiver of lien rubber stamps are available commercially.)

3. Performance bonds. Under the lien law you may protect yourself against such claims by filing (before beginning construction or improvements) an original contract for the work in the office of the county recorder and require that a contractor's payment bond be recorded in such office. Said bond shall be not less than 50 percent of the contract price and shall, in addition to any conditions for the performance of the contract, be conditioned for the payment in full of claims of all persons furnishing labor, services, equipment, or materials for the work described in the contract.

The complexity of this method deters many owner builders from using it. Some contractors resist the extra expense and trouble of posting the bond on a small job. The owner builder may find himself protected by the bond on his major subcontracts but unprotected in the areas of greatest risks, if he fails to use waiver-of-lien forms for all those not bonded.

Appendix F

Proposal — Page No. 1 of 1 Pages

WILKINSON ELECTRIC and GIFTS
Contracting - Lighting Fixtures - Household Appliances
45 West Tabernacle   St. George, Utah

PROPOSAL SUBMITTED TO	PHONE	DATE
Bill Smith		November 16, 1977

STREET	JOB NAME
509 West 600 North	Residence

CITY, STATE AND ZIP CODE	JOB LOCATION
St. George, Utah 84770	Bloomington Country Club Subdivision #

ARCHITECT	DATE OF PLANS		JOB PHONE
		Lot # 14	

We hereby submit specifications and estimates for All electrical as shown on the blue-prints. The proposal includes wiring for the following:

1. 47 Outlets
2. 26 Switches
3. 25 Lights
4. Chime from two door locations
5. Two TV locations
6. Furnish and install one smoke detector
7. Furnish and install two Nutone 9093N Heat-Vent-Lites
8. Hood
9. Range
10. Water Heaters (2)
11. Dryer
12. Nine rooms of electric radiant heat
13. Refrigerated air conditioning
14. Underground Electric Service

THANK YOU FOR THE OPPORTUNITY TO QUOTE!

We Propose hereby to furnish material and labor — complete in accordance with above specifications, for the sum of: Two Thousand--- dollars ($2,000.00)

Payment to be made as follows: $1,400.00 at the completion of the electrical rough-in with the remaining balance to be drawn when the electrical is finished.

All material is guaranteed to be as specified. All work to be completed in a workmanlike manner according to standard practices. Any alteration or deviation from above specifications involving extra costs will be executed only upon written orders, and will become an extra charge over and above the estimate. All agreements contingent upon strikes, accidents or delays beyond our control. Owner to carry fire, tornado and other necessary insurance. Our workers are fully covered by Workmen's Compensation Insurance.

Authorized Signature: *John Doe*

Note: This proposal may be withdrawn by us if not accepted within 30 days.

Acceptance of Proposal - The above prices, specifications and conditions are satisfactory and are hereby accepted. You are authorized to do the work as specified. Payment will be made as outlined above.

Signature: *Bill Smith*

Date of Acceptance _____   Signature _____

A typical electrical subcontractor's bid showing the specific items he will furnish and the work he will perform for the dollar amount shown.

PROPOSAL AND CONTRACT

TO

Date

Proposal No

Phone

PROJECT   SPECIFICATIONS:

SCOPE OF WORK:

WE PROPOSE TO FURNISH LABOR AND MATERIAL IN STRICT ACCORDANCE WITH THE PLANS AND SPECIFICATIONS AS FOLLOWS:

PRICE: FOR THE TOTAL SUM OF ...... $ _____

CONDITIONS:

It is understood and agreed that we shall not be held liable for any loss, damage or delays occasioned by fire, strikes, or material stolen after delivery upon premises, lockouts, acts of God, or the public enemy, accidents, boycotts, material shortages, disturbed labor conditions, delayed delivery of materials from Seller's suppliers, force majeure, inclement weather, floods, freight embargoes, causes incident to national emergencies, war, or other causes beyond the reasonable control of Seller, whether of like or different character, or other causes beyond his control. Prices quoted in this contract are based upon present prices and upon condition that the proposal will be accepted within thirty days. Also general conditions which are standard for specialty contractors in the construction industry.

TERMS:

Payments to be made _____ as work progresses

to the value of _____ per cent (____%) of all work completed. The entire

amount of contract to be paid within _____ days after completion.

THIS PROPOSAL IS SUBMITTED IN DUPLICATE. THE RETURN TO US OF ONE COPY WITH YOUR SIGNATURE SHALL CONSTITUTE A CONTRACT.

SUBMITTED: ACCEPTED:

By _____

Name and Registration Number of any salesperson who solicited or negotiated this contract:

Name _____ No. _____

You the buyer, may cancel this transaction at any time prior to midnight of the third business day after the date of this transaction.

Contractors are required by law to be licensed and regulated by the Contractor's State License Board. Any questions concerning a contractor may be referred to the registrar of the board whose address is: Contractor's State License Board, 1020 N Street, Sacramento, California 95814

NOTICE TO OWNER

Under the Mechanics' Lien Law, any contractor, sub-contractor, laborer, materialman or other person who helps to improve your property and is not paid for his labor, services or material, has a right to enforce his claim against your property

Under the law, you may protect yourself against such claims by filing, before commencing such work or improvement, an original contract for the work of improvement of a modification thereof, in the office of the county recorder of the county where the property is situated and requiring that a contractor's payment bond be recorded in such office. Said bond shall be in an amount not less than fifty percent (50%) of the contract price and shall, in addition to any conditions for the performance of the contract, be conditioned for the payment in full of the claims of all persons furnishing labor, services, equipment or materials for the work described in said contract.

Notice that this bid proposal and contract form calls attention to the mechanic's lien law and to California's state contractor's license law.

Appendix G

Builder's Request for Construction Advance

BUILDER'S REQUEST FOR CONSTRUCTION ADVANCE

To: State Savings & Loan
343 S. Main
Fresno, Calif.

Gentlemen:

In respect to the above referenced construction loan, we have incurred the charges for labor and material as listed on this billing, for which we hereby request checks to be prepared and disbursed.

We certify and represent that all of the labor and materials for which these bills are presented have been used in the construction of this referenced unit, and that construction to date is acceptable and is in accordance with approved plans and specifications. It is understood and agreed that the money paid under this request will be treated as trust monies and used to pay the above listed bills for labor and material.

The monies previously drawn by the undersigned in the amount of $_____ have been used to pay the labor and material bills as indicated on the Builders Requests dated _____.

_____
Borrower - Mortgagee

_____
Contractor - Builder

Item No.	Check No.	Pay to	Address	Description	Amount
			Total this Draw		
			Previous total drawn		
			Total Drawn to Date		

Loan No.	
Borrower	
Address	
Date	

Appendix H
Construction Cost Estimate

CONSTRUCTION COST ESTIMATE
WORK SHEET No. 1

Address _____
        Street   City   State   Zip

Lot No. _____ Subdivision _____ Bank or FHA No. _____

Expected start date _____ Expected completion date _____

	1 Bid or Cost	2 Name of Contractor	3 Check No.	4 Date Paid
1. Lot purchase price				
Escrow costs				
Survey and topographic map				
Percolation tests				
Electrical, water, sewer bonds				
2. Architectural fees				
3. Financing costs				
Loan application expenses				
Escrow charges				
Loan "Points"				
Title insurance				
Taxes				
Insurance (Construction and home)				
Miscellaneous charges				
4. Dept. of Building and Safety				
Building permit				
Grading permit				
Street and curb permits				
Electrical permit				
Plumbing permit				
Sewer permit				
Architectural Control fee				
Compliance and clean-up deposits				
Burning permit				
Other				
5. Equipment Rentals; materials; other minor expenses (which may not be covered in any subcontracts)				
Clean-up expenses				
Trash removal				
Portable toilet				
Temporary electrical power				
Fill dirt; top soil; hauling				
Workman's Compensation Insurance				

This page may be reproduced by photocopy for your own

CONSTRUCTION COST ESTIMATE
WORK SHEET No. 2

	Bid or Cost	Name of Contractor	Check No.	Date Paid
Subcontractors				
Excavating & Grading; dirt hauling				
Concrete - footings, foundations, slabs				
Plumbing & Sewer; septic systems				
Rough Framing; (rough carpentry)				
Trusses				
Roofing				
Airconditioning & Heating				
Electrical				
Glass & Glazing				
Windows				
Shower doors				
Mirrors				
Storm windows; screens				
Insulation				
Masonry				
Sheet Metal; soffits, fascia, rain gutters, clothes chutes, flashings				
Stucco & Plaster				
Drywall & Acoustic				
Cabinetmaker				
Finish Carpentry				
Doors - entry, passage				
Flooring - hardwood, stone, brick				
Tile (ceramic) - floors, walls, sinks				
Painting & Papering				
Carpets & Vinyl floor coverings				
Drapes, shutters, shades				
Finish Grading				
Fencing				
Landscaping				
Automatic Sprinkling system				
Finish Concrete - driveway, sidewalks, patios, planters				
Solar Water Heater				
Domestic Water Well				
Kitchen Appliances				
Range				
Ovens - Microwave; standard wall				
Exhaust hoods				
Garbage disposal				
Dishwasher				
Trash compactor				
Sinks, faucets				
Water purifier (filter system)				
Intercom. system				

This page may be reproduced by photocopy for your own use.

CONSTRUCTION COST ESTIMATE
WORK SHEET No. 3

	Bid or Cost	Name of Contractor	Check No.	Date Paid
8. Laundry Room Appliances				
Washer and Dryer				
Laundry sink				
Water heaters				
Water softener				
Central vacuum system				
9. Bathroom Fixtures (may be included in subcontracts)				
Toilets				
Tubs				
Surrounds (tile, cultured onyx, etc.)				
Showers (pre-fab.; glass; tiled)				
Lavatories (individual, or cast in counter top)				
Medicine chests				
Mirrors, towel bars, faucets, etc.				
10. Lighting Fixtures				
Exterior - garage, entry, yard				
Foyer (entrance hall)				
Halls				
Dining room				
Kitchen - drop ceiling, other				
Bedrooms				
Bathrooms				
Living room				
Laundry; stairways; basement				
11. Carpets & Vinyl floors (If not contracted)				
12. Misc. Items (that might not be included in any contract.)				
Wrought iron railings				
Steel beams and columns				
Entry door hardware; passage knobs				
Garage door; automatic door opener				
Total all costs				
Contingency ___ %				
Total Estimated Cost of Project				

This page may be reproduced by photocopy for your own use

Index

Building, inspecting for remodeling, 1-2
Cleaning up and disposing of rubbish during remodeling, 3
Construction advance, sample of builder's request for, 96
Contract form, sample, 94
Contracting for alterations, 8
Cost control: construction progress draws, 89-90; lien waiver, 90-92 simplified accounting system, 89;
Cost estimate form, construction, sample of, 98-100
Cost estimating for additions, 7; for alterations, 8; for remodeling, 3-4
Cost estimating for new house: accuracy, 29; how to develop, 30; contingency percentage, 30; determining total cost of project, 30-31
Cost-plus agreements for remodeling, 4
Demolition, estimating costs of, 2-3
Designing additions, 7
Expenses, avoiding the unexpected, 11-12
Financing for additions, 7; for alterations, 8; for remodeling, 5
Financing: draws during progress of construction, 19-20; getting acquainted with lending institutions, 17; getting the best loan, 17-18; presenting the project, 19
Getting ready for construction, first steps in, 9
Glossary of common construction terms, 85-88

Insurance: builder's risk, 71; for alterations, 8; liability, 71; owner-builder as employer, 73; title, 71; what and why, 71; workman's compensation, 72-73
Location, selecting for your lot, 11
Lot purchase agreement form, 14
Permits, building: for large cities and heavily populated counties, 76-78; for small cities and counties, 76; how to apply for, 75; sample instructions for, 79-81; working with inspectors, 75
Plans, house, details of: basement and foundation, 25; detail sheets, 25; floor, 24; front, side and rear elevations, 25; general specifications, 25-26; plot, 24; window and door schedules, 25
Plans, house: checking, 27; sources, 21-22; what should be included, 23-26; working with architect, 22-23
Prearrangements, construction, 59
Reconstruction during remodeling, 6
Remodeling, 1
Reusable items, storing and protecting during remodeling, 3, 5
Schedule, construction: chronological outline, 56-57; daily activities, 59-68
Subcontractors, searching for: as long-time resident of area, 47-48; desirable qualities, 49; evaluating bids and selecting, 52-54; in large cities, 48; in medium-sized communities, 48; obtaining bids, 50-52;

reference information, 49-50
Subcontractors, types and activities:
cabinentmaker, 44; concrete, 34; plumbing, 34-39; definition, 33; drywall, 44; electrical, 41-42; excavating and grading, 33; finish carpentry, 40-41; framing carpentry, 39-40; glass and glazing, 43; heating and air conditioning, 37, 38, 41; insulation, 43; masonry, 42; miscellaneous, 45; painting, 44-45; sewer, sewer tank, septic tank and cesspool, 36, 38; sheet metal, 42-43; stucco and plaster, 43-44; water well, 38

Subcontractors: keeping file cards on, 83-84; sample bids, 93

Tearing down during remodeling, 3, 5

Terms, glossary of, 85-88

Weather protection during remodeling, 5

Weather protection for additions, 7